东京手艺人

手作传统工艺的守护者

[日] Beretta P-05 著
杜海清 译

文匯出版社

写在前面的话

那些能工巧匠矢志坚守并一直传承至今的传统、技艺、美感，还有精神……

不管时代如何变迁，我们总还是希望能有代代相传的东西。

策划本书的意图正在于此。

不知您是否知道，在东京都，被指定为传统工艺品的共涉及40个业种。入选传统工艺品的标准非常严格，比如要求大部分是手工制作；采用的传统技术、工艺的历史得在一百年以上；必须使用传统的生产原料；东京都内至少要有四家企业在进行生产等。

为此，我们派出了一批锐意进取的年轻摄影师，对东京都指定的40种传统工艺，以及从事相关制作的49位手艺人进行多次跟踪采访、拍摄，最终汇集成您眼前的这本书。

这些能工巧匠坚持此行数十年，他们不是囿于传统不思进取，而是精益求精，不断打磨技艺，淬炼精神，制作出做工精细、堪称完美的工艺品。通过摄影师们深情的拍摄，您还能一睹这些手艺人不为人知的一面——在一般人无法看到的生产现场，当他们全身心投入制作时不时流露出的认真、可爱的表情……

有人说，传统工艺制作现在正面临着后继乏人、相关业者纷纷改行的严峻局面，但我们相信，只要这些能工巧匠凝聚心血制作出来的优质“珍品”还在，那么，流传至今的古老工艺一定能代代相传。

对于传统工艺品，若不是亲手接触、使用，便无法体会到它独特的魅力。所以我们希望读者不只是满足于摄影师拍出的照片，还要去实际接触摄影师亲眼所见、切身感受到的真正的传统工艺世界。

但愿本书能成为这些传统得以坚守、传承的一点助力。

多摩织

东京手染浴衣

江户和竿

东京画框

东京刀具

江户花布染

目录

MURAYAMA OSHIMA TSUMUGI
村山大岛捻线绸

村山大岛捻线绸诞生于江户时代后期。村山大岛捻线绸作为丝织品进行生产的时间大概在1920年前后。它是由“正蓝染”的棉织品村山绀絣（绀絣：在藏青底色上织出碎白道花纹——译者注）和“玉茧”的丝织品砂川太织（太织：用粗线织成的丝织品，即粗线绸子——译者注）合并而成。

村山大岛捻线绸最显著的特点，一是光泽柔和、手感舒适；二是具有民间工艺风格和纯绢的典雅感；三是它没有正反面之分。

这些独特的优点赢得了口碑。1967年，村山大岛捻线绸被列为东京都指定非物质文化遗产；1975年被日本经济产业省认定为传统工艺品。

Murayama Oshima-tsumugi craftsmanship weaves silk and cotton cloth into superb kimono, hapi, haori jackets and other traditional Japanese textile artistry. From the time Oshima-tsumugi silk kimonos first appeared in what is now Tokyo toward the end of the Edo Period, they have been known for their glossy look, smooth feel, traditional, refined taste, and signature either-direction fabric designs that can be worn front or back. In 1967, the Tokyo Metropolitan Government declared Oshima-tsumugi woven goods an intangible cultural asset.

制作村山大岛捻线绸大致要经过九道工序，
图为在第七道工序“印染”上专心致志工作的田代先生。

❖ 田房染织有限会社

田代隆久

还在念书的时候，田代隆久先生就对制作纺织品抱有兴趣，并开始入行。他师从父亲田代悦康学手艺，那时父亲是村山大岛捻线绸传统工艺师，现在已去世。1990年，田代隆久先生继承了家业—田房染织有限会社。1994年，村山大岛捻线绸的制作技术得到认可，他获得了国家传统工艺师资格。田代隆久先生一直抱着要将日本文化传给后代的强烈愿望，埋头从事着自己的工作。现在，他们一方面将村山大岛捻线绸与众不同的优越之处发扬光大，另一方面又不拘泥于既成观念，大胆开展创新创造活动。

Takahisa Tashiro, Tokyo's leading Oshima-tsumugi craftsman, began developing his lifelong interest in fabric and clothing construction as a schoolboy, when he started at the family kimono weaving factory. Tutored in the textile arts by his artisan father, he took over the kimono business in 1965. The Tokyo Metropolitan Government officially recognized his mastery in 1994, when it named him a certified Traditional Craftsman.

田房染织有限会社

◯ 东京都武藏村山市三木2-46-1

Photo/押尾晓子

TOKYO SOMEKOMON
东京染小纹

染小纹，意即碎花印染，它的历史可追溯到室町时代。进入江户时代后，人们开始在武士的礼服上印染碎花，于是，碎花印染进入了正式的发展轨道。碎花印染要经过刻制纸样、调制色糊、在布料上印染花纹、染底色、水蒸、漂洗、干燥等多道工序。

到了江户时代中期，碎花印染工艺在民间开始普及，经过不断创新改良，制作的产品越来越漂亮，直至今日风格更为洗练。“东京染小纹”这一名称，意指它是在东京用锥子和小刀刻制花样并进行印染的。

Tokyo some-komon (fine-pattern stencil dyeing) uses traditional Japanese stencils to create dotted patterns of extremely fine detail. These pinpoint stencil patterns were first used in warriors' formal dress called kamishiro during in the Muromachi Period. Later, in the middle of the Edo Period, some-komon patterns became more widely used by common people. The fine-pattern stencil dyes are seen today in women's "visiting" kimonos.

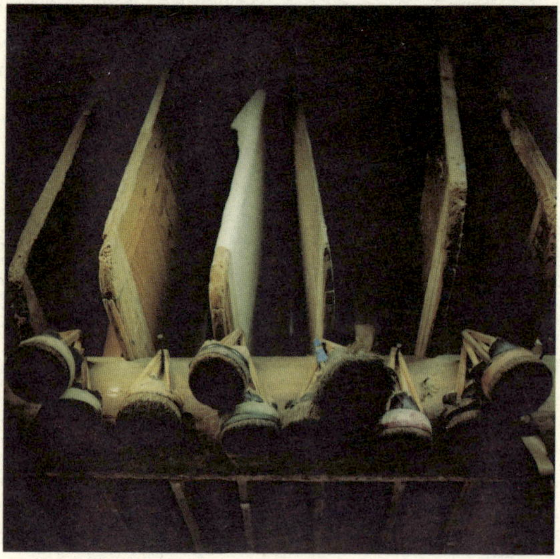

柿渋

❖ 富田染工艺纸型印染部

佐藤勇三

创始于1914年的老字号“富田染工艺”的纸型印染部由佐藤勇三先生（艺名：佐藤雄山）一手负责。佐藤先生拥有40多年的工作经验，其熟稔的手艺已到了炉火纯青的地步。作为传统工艺师，他肩负着发展东京都新中心新宿本地产业的重任，将这一起始于江户时代的传统技艺及其精湛感觉传承至今。近期作品有以“日本三景”为题材的“安艺的宫岛”等。

In 1914 the venerable dyehouse Tomita Somekogei moved to specialize in katazome, a design form in which sticky ingredients are pushed through a stencil to define a pattern. Yuzan Sato, the current Tomita Somekogei dye master, produces elegant work borne of his 40-year plus career. As the latest in a line of traditional craftsmen in one of Shinjuku's key local industries, he keeps both the techniques and sense of style from the Edo Period alive in modern-day Japan.

富田染工艺

东京都新宿区西早稻田3-6-14
03-3987-0701

Photo/奥田善彦

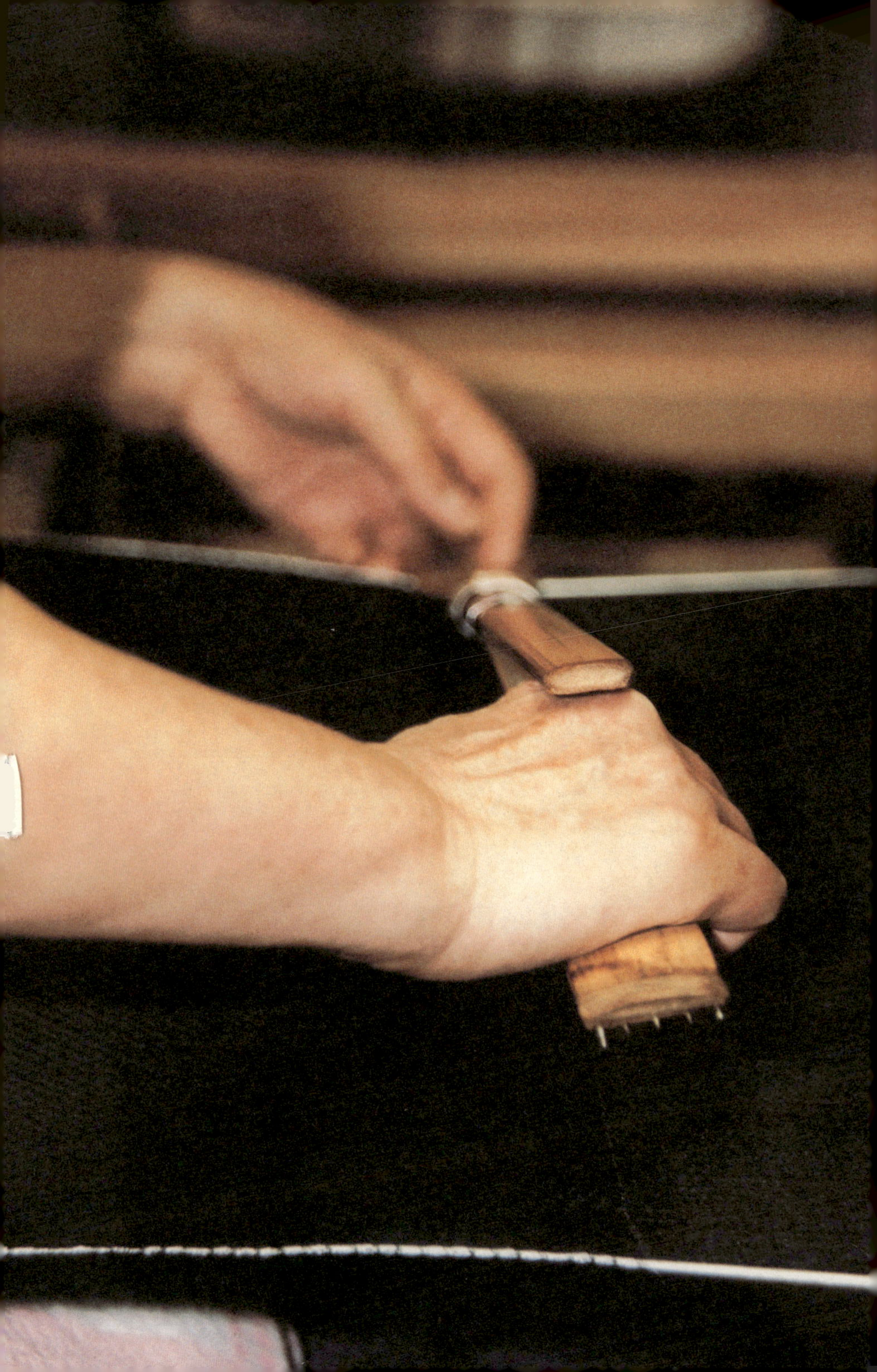

HONBA KIHACHIJO
原产黄八丈

黄八丈是八丈岛的传统丝织品，据说八丈岛就是因它命名。1977年被指定为日本传统工艺品；1984年，山下MEYU先生被指定为东京都“非物质文化遗产”继承者。制作黄八丈，先是以生长于八丈岛上的草木作为天然染料，染成黄、桦（偏红的黄色）、黑三种颜色的丝线，然后将丝线绞在一起，用手工织成竖纹、格纹等各种花样的丝织品。

黄八丈的特点是历经多年不会变色，反而随着洗涤次数的增多色彩越发鲜艳。

Kihachijo cloth, named after Hachijo Island, is an elegant dyed fabric for traditional kimono and obi, which was designated a Traditional Handicraft by the Ministry of Economy, Trade and Industry in 1977. In creating kihachijo, the dyestuff is extracted from dried island vegetation known as kobunagusa and transferred to thread, which is then hand-woven into the final cloth. Renowned for its colorfastness, the kihachijo coloration becomes more vivid the more it is washed.

❖ 黄八丈MEYU工房

山下誉/山下芙美子

漂染工艺师山下誉先生染出的色彩十分鲜艳，彻底颠覆了人们对草木染的印象。为了继承黄八丈的染织传统，并将其传给后世，山下誉先生一边在大学担任临时讲师，一边在工坊间向造访八丈岛的游客讲授黄八丈的工艺知识。妻子芙美子是一位纺织工艺师，母亲山下MEYU则是东京都的“非物质文化遗产”继承者。纺织这个活很复杂，手脚协调配合的好坏决定了织物质量的优劣，容不得半点马虎；而丝线的配色和花样设计也需要相当的审美能力，织就的绸料必是毫无缝隙的完美成品。若用如此高贵的绸料来制作普通穿着的和服，未免会有大材小用的感觉。

Dye master Homare Yamashita oversees the dyeing process at the kihachijo workshop where the cloth is produced. His technique helps fabrics achieve a rich, brilliant coloration that takes natural plant dyeing to a new level. The weaver, Fumiko Yamashita, then spins the kimono fabric to life. Together, they produce sophisticated color patterns and designs for products characterized by their perfect workmanship. Their mother, Meyu Yamashita, possesses a level of expertise so high that the Tokyo Metropolitan Government has declared her skills an intangible cultural asset.

黄八丈MEYU工房

东京都八丈岛八丈町中之乡2542

04996-7-0411

Photo/古宫美纪

EDO KIMEKOMININGYO
江户贴花人偶

公元1740年前后，一位为京都上贺茂神社制作“供献箱”的匠人，将多余的碎料做出了贴花人偶，这便是江户贴花人偶的起始。手艺高超的匠人先在木质的人偶身体上刻出条痕，然后再贴上锦缎绉绸等外衣，所以称之为“贴花人偶”；而江户贴花人偶，是指采用这种工艺手法制作的人偶在江户一带流传。

江户贴花人偶除了用木料制作外，现在也有用桐塑材料制作的，有的人偶头和手脚还用上了素瓷等材料。

A craftsman serving in a shrine in Kyoto around 1740 created items such as wooden boxes for monetary offerings, and saved the leftover wood. He used the willow wood scraps to carve the first kimekomi-literally, tuck-in-dolls. After creating the doll body, edges of fabric material are tucked in to the grain of the wood from which the little doll is carved. This unique doll-making technique eventually spread to Edo, where it was popularized as the Edo kimekomi style.

❖ 株式会社柿沼人形

柿沼正志

柿沼正志先生1948年9月出生在东京，自1974年师从父亲柿沼东光后，便专心于人偶制作。1999年，他被认定为“通产大臣认定传统工艺师”；2000年被认定为“东京都知事认定传统工艺师”。色彩高贵华丽的皇子、设计独特的男童节人偶等作品不断问世。他获奖无数，曾三次获得内阁总理大臣奖，四次获得通产大臣奖，一次获得东京都知事奖，如今仍在不停地创作。

Masashi Kakinuma, one of today's greatest doll-making masters, learned the trade from his father and began specializing in kimekomi in 1974. By 1999, he was certified a Traditional Craftsman by the Minister of Economy, Trade and Industry, followed a year later with similar recognition from the Governor of Tokyo. His uniquely designed and beautifully colored dolls have been displayed in a succession of exhibitions, winning numerous awards.

株式会社柿沼人形

东京都荒川区西尾久2-1-5
048-964-7877
www.kakinuma-ningyo.com
kakinuma-ningyo@nifty.com

Photo/水岛大介 Assistant/寒河江怜子

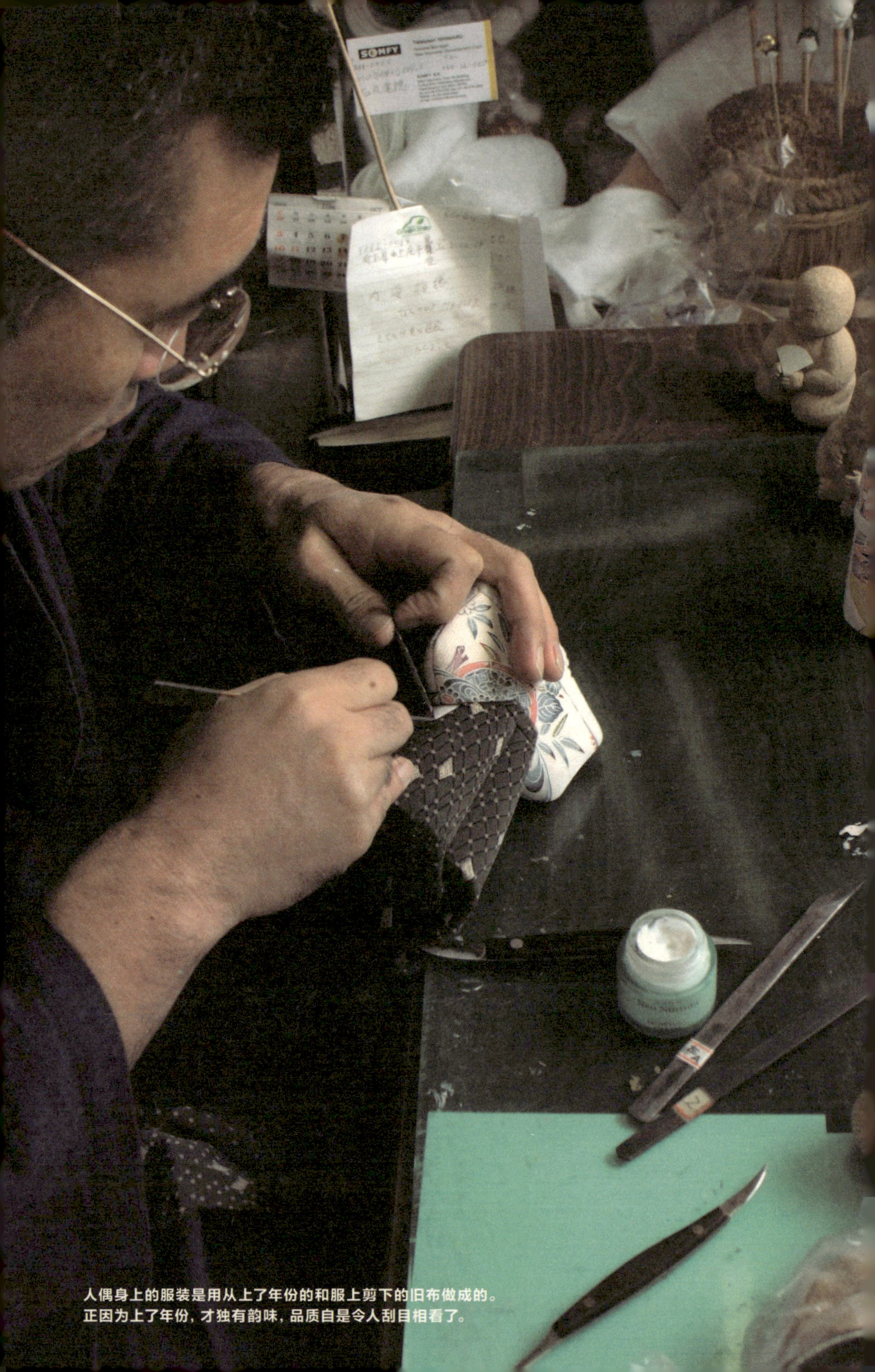

人偶身上的服装是用从上了年份的和服上剪下的旧布做成的。
正因为上了年份，才独有韵味，品质自是令人刮目相看了。

EDO KIMEKOMININGYO
江户贴花人偶

江户时代中期诞生于京都，随后传至江户，在这个过程中种类日趋多样化、制作日益精细化，形成了今天的江户贴花人偶。制作贴花人偶，先是用桐塑（浆糊拌入桐木锯屑制作而成）做成人偶的坯型，然后再在坯型上刻上细细的条痕，贴上布料。江户贴花人偶的坯型多种多样，可以任由匠人在上面充分施展自己的技艺，彰显个性风格。人偶虽小，品格各异，常被用作三月三女儿节人偶、干支人偶等，深受人们喜爱。

Today's kimekomi doll figures are usually made of sawdust blended with jute fiber and glue. Silk brocade or other varieties of cloth are glued and tucked into the grooves of the body to produce the final doll. Although the craft is imbued with a sense of tradition and prestige, it also gives each craftsman free play in expressing his skill, artistry, and individuality, since the doll pattern is different for every kimekomi. The dolls are favorites for hina-ningyo Girls' Festival displays.

约手掌大小的女儿节人偶是一件非常逗人喜爱的名品。

❖ 塚田工房

塚田进

1949年出生在墨田区的塚田进先生是一位著名的人偶制作工艺师（雅号：咏春），他同时被认定为东京都传统工艺师和通商产业大臣传统工艺师，这是很少见的。与此同时，他还是一位制作人偶坯型的行家。“如果不能够从头至尾把握人偶制作的全道工序，你就无法赋予人偶以灵魂。”正是本着这样的理念，从坯型制作到最后完成，每道工序他都能一个人应对自如。直到现在，他仍孜孜不倦地学习制作各种人偶，意在充分发挥贴花技术，创作出富有个性的人偶。

Born in Tokyo's Sumida Ward in 1949, Susumu Tsukada went on to become a premiere doll-making artist and craftsman, one of very few recognized as a Traditional Craftsman by both the Ministry of Economy, Trade and Industry and the Tokyo Metropolitan Government. He continues working to bring his expertise to life in his dolls, the embodiment of his unique aesthetic vision.

塚田工房

东京都墨田区向岛2-11-7
TEL：03-3622-4579
www.edokimekomi.com

Photo/伊藤尚子

TOKYO GINKI
东京银器

江户时代中期，雕刻师横谷宗明对本地手艺人的制作工具进行革新，改进了技术和手法，这便是东京银器的滥觞。叮叮当当敲击一块金属板，或延伸或缩小，这种被称作“锻金”的手法可以让一块金属板立体成型；然后再进行一些必要的装饰，做成的制品就是东京银器了。

敲打金属板时发出的悦耳声响在作坊内回荡，叮叮当当的声响中，一块银质的板材便渐渐变成了一件没有任何接口、浑然天成的器物。

Tokyo silver work (ginki) started with engraver Somin Yokoya. He pioneered what was then breakthrough smithing technology to produce utensils for the townsfolk in the mid-Edo Period. Tokyo silver work involves hammering out sheet metal, then shrinking it in a plating process, a traditional method referred to as tankin. The tankin style allows molding and decorating the metal in the same process.

❖ 东浦银器制作所

石黑光南

内里衬上一块凸状的金属物件，然后用凹状的槌子在表面上一粒一粒地敲打出像“霰”一样的突出物。这种称之为“霰打”的手艺，只有光南（本名：照雄）等三个人才掌握。干这个活需要专心致志，所以，“霰打”通常是在深更半夜由他一个人做。白天，作坊间里虽然只有6个弟子在“叮叮当当”，但据说还有很多人在排队等着做他的徒弟。制作银器用的工具也是匠人自己制造的。作坊间里一长溜放着匠人们从父辈手上接过的各种工具。

Few if any artisans can match the silver handiwork of Konan Ishiguro, but many would like to try. At present, there are six apprentices working under him, but the waiting list for the position is longer. Ishiguro creates his own silversmith's tools, which rest next to the set he inherited from his father in the workshop.

东浦银器制作所

- 文京区弥生2-20-6
- 03-3813-2241
- 光南陈列室：东京都文京区根津1-17-6谷川大楼 1F
- 03-5814-2035

Photo/鸭志田顺子

天神印白墨

TOKYO TEGAKI YUZEN
东京手绘友禅

友禅染最早是在江户时代享保年间（1684-1687年）由京都画家宫崎友禅斋创制的。

到了江户时代的文化、文政时期（1804-1827年），友禅染的创作手法也就跟随着“出京物品”（江户时期对来自京都、大阪的高档物品的统称——译者注）一起，从关西地区传入了以武家政治为中心，文化、经济俱荣的江户。

手绘友禅传到江户后，相对于京都的雅致，在图案和色调上，更倾向于时尚和古雅趣味，成就了今天的东京手绘友禅。

The tegaki yuzen method of drawing elaborate designs on silk is named for Yuzensai Miyazaki, the Kyoto painter who perfected the style during the Edo Period. This dyeing technique migrated from Kansai to Edo along with the commodities it decorated. Edo aesthetic sensibilities were reflected in chic, sophisticated designs, a divergence from the Kyoto miyabi conception of elegance that had informed the style to that time. Hand-drawn patterns with this more colorful flair came to be known as Tokyo tegaki yuzen.

❖ 染之高孝

高桥孝之

高桥孝之是东京都工艺染色协会常务理事。高桥的作坊有各种车间，所有印染作业均可进行。除了手绘友禅外，也可进行江户花布、一珍染、木纹染、波纹染（仿大理石花纹印染——译者注）等，以制作和服、腰带为主，兼及西服衣料。高桥的作坊是东京唯一一家使用“一珍糊”（用小麦粉做成的浆糊）的印染手工作坊，其最具魅力之处在于，能制作迥然于京友禅、加贺友禅的个性独特的作品。

Takayuki Takahashi, a tegaki yuzen artist, is also a second-generation member of the Tokyo Tegaki Yuzen Executive Board. In addition to the tegaki yuzen, his prolific workshop produces obi and kimono with Edo sarasa style dyed silk, as well as icchin zome designs. Of the techniques the studio employs, the icchin flour paste dyeing is perhaps the most unusual-only one workshop in Tokyo is using it. The individual personality reflected in each piece is the key source of attraction running through the variety of production methods and artifacts.

染之高孝

东京都新宿区高田马场3-9-1

03-3368-7388

Photo/今井大子

“咚咚卡拉卡拉”，日夜响个不停的机杼声替代了摇篮曲，伴随着他长大成人，继承家业。织成一反（布匹长度单位：约宽34厘米，长10米——译者注）多摩织费时约一个月。

TAMAORI
多摩织

多摩织是在多摩川流域和八王子市、秋留野市一带流传的传统工艺。上述这些地方过去曾被称为“桑都”，一直出产着品种繁多的丝绸品，以满足江户地区多样化的需要。

如今，有御召织、捻线绸织、风通织、变缀、捩织等五个种类被指定为多摩织。用多摩织做成的衣物穿在身上，有越穿越舒服的感觉。从前，不仅是东京平民居住区的妇人，连一流的艺人也爱将多摩织做成的和服当作日常穿着的衣物。用高档的丝绸织成的和服看似不经意地穿在身上，却是由里而外透出一股时尚味儿。

Tamaori (Tama fabric work) is the generic name for the traditional handicraft centered in Akiruno-shi, Hachioji, encompassing five different types of weave: omeshiori, tsumugiori, futsuori, kawaritsuzure, and mojiriori. Stylistically, these range from intricate tapestries to pre-twisted woven cloths, twills, and more complex satin weaves. Tamaori kimonos are durable, and get more and more comfortable with every wearing. They have traditionally been considered the height of sophisticated fashion, favored by the top geisha.

多摩织采用生丝作为原料，其特点是要经过“先练”（精练提纯，去除杂质）、“先染”（对原丝先染再织）等工序。

❖ 有限会社泽井织物工场

泽井荣一郎

泽井荣一郎先生1921年出生，从祖父一代算起，从事多摩织生产已是第三代。从战场上归来后，他回到家乡，用仅存的3台织机继承家业。他在顾客眼光挑剔的银座、新桥开设专卖店，在满足较高消费需求的同时，不断提高传统技术水平，努力改进产品，提高品质。不会出现折痕、膝盖处时间长了不会变薄的多摩织和服，穿在身上行动自如，因而大受顾客好评。他家生产的多摩织和服，还时常用于能乐、歌舞伎等传统艺术表演。泽井家族里有多位艺术家，携手为弘扬多摩织的传统做出贡献。

Eiichiro Sawai, a third-generation master weaver, was born in 1921. He returned from the war to take over the family business, successfully building it back into a thriving kimono factory from the three looms remaining at war's end. Wrinkle-free, comfortable Tama kimonos have always been renowned for the ease of movement they offer. They are often used in traditional performances such as noh and kabuki.

有限会社泽井织物工场

东京都八王子市高月町1181
0426-91-1032

Photo/松原容子

TOKYO KUMIHIMO
东京编织丝带

编织丝带（用丝线或棉线编织而成的绳带——译者注）的历史悠久，其用途也是多种多样，除了用来捆绑、结扎物品，打结的方法、绳结的颜色和绳结的配置，还常被用来表示吉凶、性别、身份等。即使到了现在，日本人的日常生活中还经常使用编织丝带，如和服腰带上的带扣、用在和服外褂上的“羽织纽”等。

东京编织丝带最初是用在铠甲上的，所以两根丝带相交后结扎的绳纽最富特点，能结扎得非常牢固。另外，对素雅色彩的偏好，也是时髦的江户风格之象征。

The art of kumihimo braiding traces back more than a thousand years. Over that period, artisans and craftsmen have developed a wide diversity of uses beyond merely securing and fastening objects. In its decorative role, the position and color of the kumihimo have historically been used to symbolize gender, indicate the rank of officials-even tell fortunes. The braids remain a part of everyday life in Japan today, serving as obijime to secure the obi sashes worn with kimono, or as short cords to fasten haori jackets in the front.

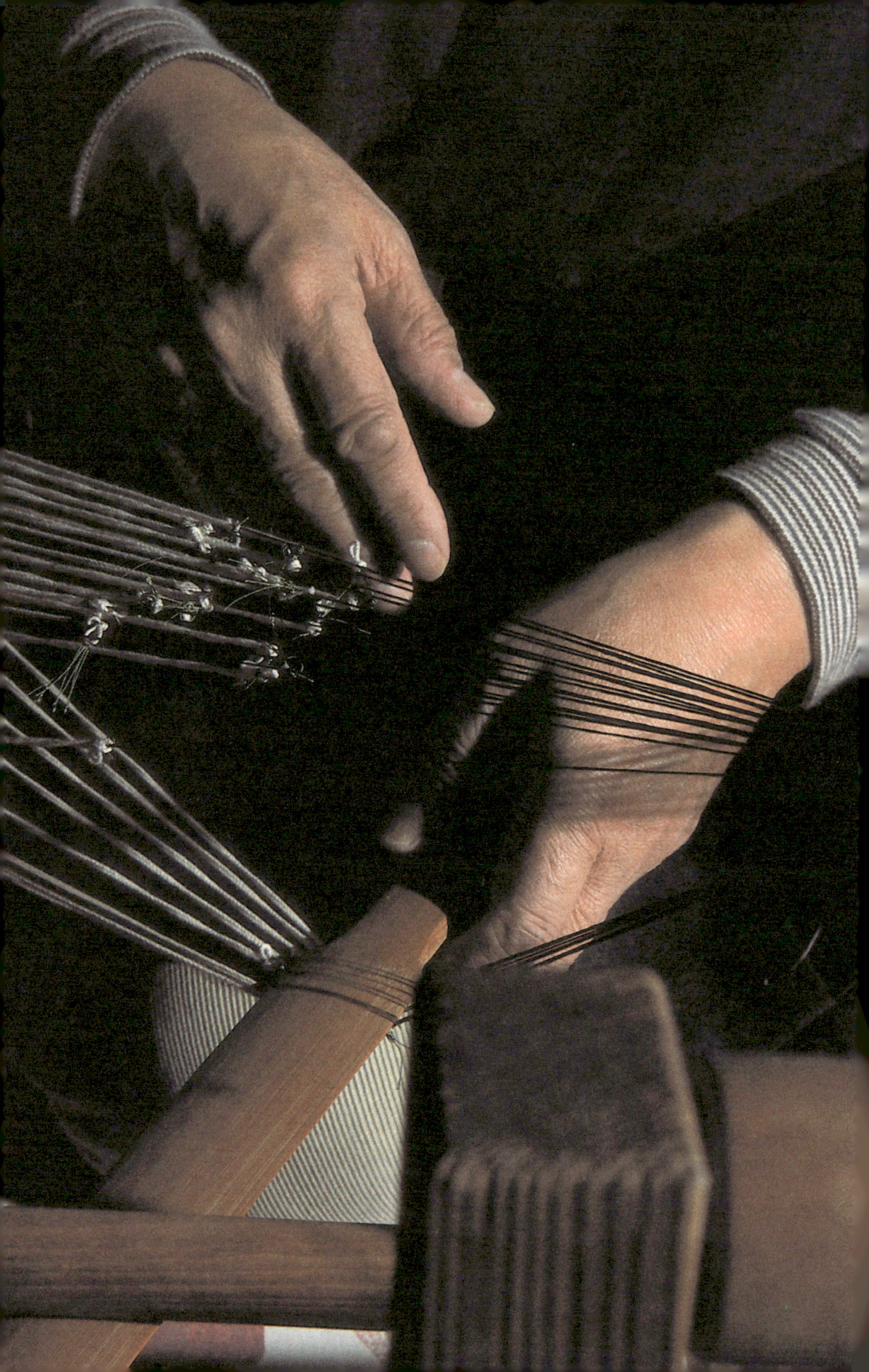

❖ 横塚纽工艺

横塚石凤

横塚石凤先生一方面作为丝带工艺师专注于丝带的制作，另一方面还在博物馆当讲师，致力于丝带制作的实际演示、指导，将日本的传统工艺传给下一代。此外，他还从学术的角度进行考证，对用于铠兜上的丝带的种类、技艺、制作方法进行研究，力图再现这一传统技艺的风貌。总之，只要与传统丝带相关的，他都倾注了极大的热情。遵循东京编织丝带的传统，并以独特的美感制作而成的丝带，不单是服装上的配角，若是充当主角也毫不逊色。

As one of the nation's most accomplished braiders, kumihimo master Sekiho Yokotsuka naturally spends a great deal of time making the kumihimo artifacts himself, but he is also an ardent advocate for the craft, offering lectures and demonstrations at venues including museums, and sharing his expertise in support of other aspiring artisans. As a researcher and academic, he is absorbed in the study of the different types of kumihimo incorporated in the armor of Japan's ancient warriors, and the techniques and processes used to make them. Thus, the braider finds himself completely interwoven in a passionate relationship with his art.

横塚纽工艺

埼玉县岩槻市本町1-14-4
048-758-5553

Photo/古宫美纪

EDO SHIKKI
江户漆器

江户漆器是日常生活中常见的工艺品，比如套盒、饭桌、木碗等。江户设府的时候，德川家康汇聚了一批京都来的工匠，让他们生产日常用的物品，这便有了江户漆器的说法。英语中“Japan”一词的另一个含义就是漆器，可见它是日本有着悠久历史的独特的工艺品。

制作漆器大致要经过七道工序。踏实、细致的操作连贯进行、一气呵成，一件漆器精品的问世，离不开制作者高超的技艺和不急不躁的耐心。

Edo shikki is a type of lacquerwork widely used to finish bowls, trays, boxes and chopsticks. So intimately associated with the spirit of the nation is this lacquer craft that it is known in English as "japan." A variety of techniques exist for building up the lacquer, but since they all require the delicate-and patient-application of layer upon layer, it is the artisan's perseverance as well as his craftsmanship that produces a true shikki gem, a masterful embodiment of the art.

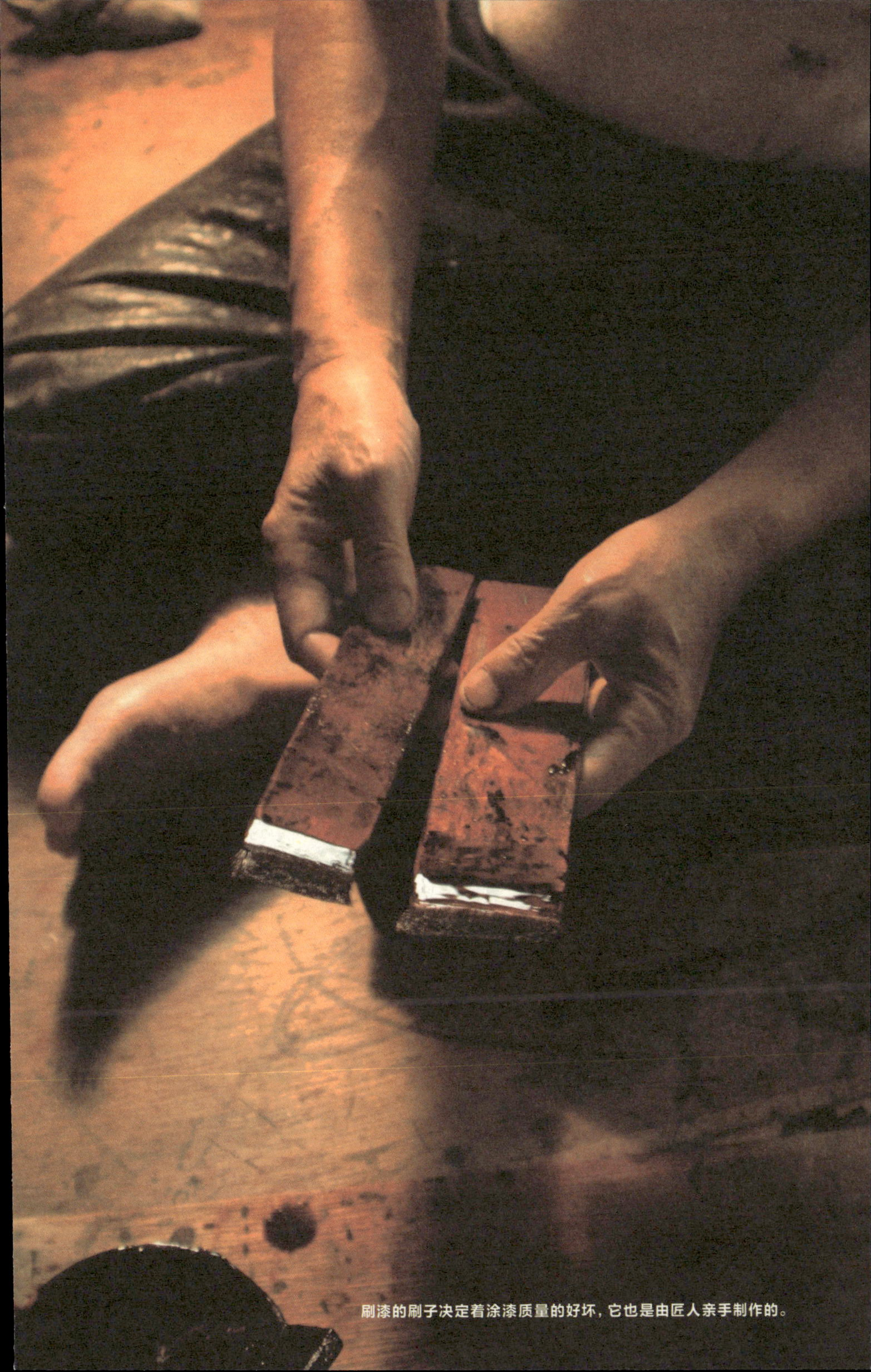

刷漆的刷子决定着涂漆质量的好坏，它也是由匠人亲手制作的。

道
8 9 10
15 16 17 18 19 20
22 23 24 25 26 27 28
29 30 31

❖ 白石漆器

白石敏道

白石敏道先生是一位专长于涂漆的工艺师。他也许是东京最后一位真正懂得日常生活富含着真谛的手艺人了。他并不把自己视为艺术家，而只是一名工匠，所以他从不在作品上留下自己的姓名。“涂漆是无限的，不拘于形状，所以它可以应用于任何物品上。”从26岁开始独立创业后，他已用了48年的涂漆台上那一层一层的漆，仿佛同白石先生的人生重叠在了一起。

After plying the shikki craft for some time, one of the nation's top artisans, Toshimichi Shiraishi, set out on his own at the age of 26. In describing his attraction to shikki, he points out that "Lacquer is an infinitely variable medium. It can be applied not only to decorate but actually create a wide variety of objects." Layering lacquer-glued paper to the interior of a mold produces rich colored surfaces that can be further polished and decorated. No simple paint can do that.

白石漆器

东京都葛饰区四木3-2-5

03-5671-2346

Photo/伊藤明子

EDO BEKKO
江户玳瑁

富有光泽的条纹，琥珀色的怡人色调，柔滑的肌肤触感，让人感受到一种纯天然的温暖感觉。据说，用这种材料制作的梳子和发簪，使用时能吸收头部的热量，从而缓解头疼等头部不适症状。

早在公元607年，玳瑁制品就由遣唐使从中国传到日本。后来到了江户时代又增加了新的技术，成为价格昂贵的装饰品，受到人们的青睐。江户玳瑁制品不用任何粘合剂，而是以水和热压的方式进行粘合，这是日本独有的技术。由技术熟练的手艺人制作的玳瑁工艺品，若是保养得当，据说可以保存一两百年。

Smooth to the touch, with flashes of amber coursing through their characteristic light patterns, Edo bekko tortoise shell artifacts are as attractive as they are distinct. Legend has it that bekko used for women's hair ornaments and combs offers medicinal benefit as well as aesthetic merit, absorbing heat from the head and relieving headaches. Historically, bekko crafts were introduced from China by returning Japanese envoys to the Sui Dynasty in 607. Yet relatively few articles become antiques: artifacts produced by tortoise shell craftsmen are said to remain functional for 100-even 200-years.

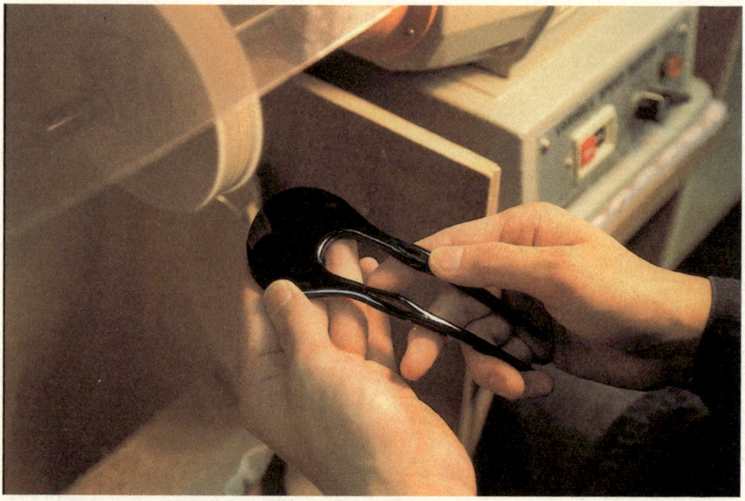

凭着独有的灵感和熟稔的技艺，专注于每一道工序。

上图／将削得薄薄的几片玳瑁重合在一起，不用粘合剂，这种“压制合成”的技术难度最大。
下图／加工玳瑁所用的工具大多是匠人自己制作的，也会使用天然的草木。

在最后一道切削工序中，手不能直接触及玳瑁，不然玳瑁沾到手上的油渍，30年后会出现色斑。

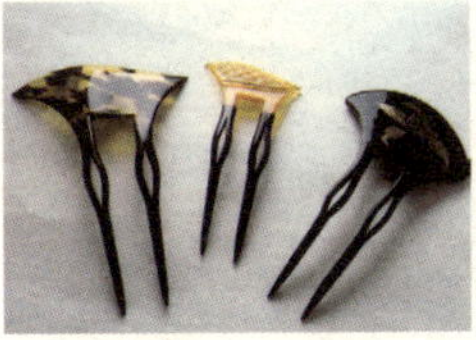 

❖ 鳖甲矶贝

矶贝实

矶贝实先生91岁的父亲矶贝库太是资深工艺师、文化勋章获得者。矶贝实先生在父亲的手下刻苦钻研，在2002年被指定为江东区的“非物质文化遗产”继承者。他的三个儿子矶贝克实、矶贝刚、矶贝大辅，原先选择了不同的发展道路，现在也都成了振兴“鳖甲矶贝”的可靠接班人。矶贝实先生十分活跃，曾随文化使节团访问过法国、俄罗斯、葡萄牙等国家，在国内外获得很高的评价。他还在高中、文化机构担任讲师，致力于传播玳瑁文化。他说：“如今这个时代，匠人如果只是埋头制作,总有一天会走向没落；除了制作产品外，还得有创新思维和活动能力。”

Schooled in the craft by his father Kota-himself an Order of Cultural Merit recipient-Minoru Isogai's talent was recognized by the government of Japan with an Intangible Cultural Asset designation in 2002. Today he is internationally acclaimed for his demonstrations of the craft overseas, while at home he is working to pass down the bekko tradition by lecturing at high schools and cultural facilities throughout Japan, among other activities.

鳖甲矶贝

东京都江东区龟户3-3-6

03-5628-1244

Photo/和田京子

作坊就在自己家的宅地内，基本上都是坐着工作。

EDO HAKE
江户毛刷

毛刷是涂刷物品的工具。如今，有经师毛刷、染色毛刷、人偶毛刷、油漆毛刷等总共七种毛刷被指定为“江户毛刷”。制作毛刷所用的材料，如人的毛发，马、鹿、羊等动物的毛，棕榈等，用途不同，材料各异，全凭毛刷工艺师一双火眼金睛来进行挑选。

毛刷的精髓在于毛梢。用起来“涂刷均匀”“有筋道”，就被认为是质量过得硬的毛刷。所以，制作毛刷的大部分工序都花在了梳理毛梢、修直用毛及去除用毛上的油脂等上面。

Hake paintbrushes are used primarily for the application of delicate watercolors. They may be made of any of a number of materials, including human hair, horsehair, and deer, sheep or goat hair, with the actual selection based on the intended application, and the discerning eye of the brushmaker. The tip is crucial: to be considered an excellent hake brush, it should have sufficient body to allow the ink or watercolor to flow properly from the belly of the brush to the tip, without any excess remaining after the stroke is completed.

制作毛刷不可缺少的刀具，已用旧了的刀具似乎在诉说它悠长的历史。

为了方便使用，手柄部分要仔细打磨。

制作毛刷最重要且难度最大的工序“梳理用毛”，要剔除断头的毛和倒竖的毛。

❖ 小林刷毛制作所

田中重己

田中重己先生入行40年左右，已是制作毛刷的高手。他初中毕业后便跟随父亲学这门手艺。与此同时他也不放松深造，在高中和大学的夜校学习化学。如今，他正致力于将学到的化学知识用在革新传统的制作工艺上，推出新的毛刷产品。

Shigemi Tanaka has been making hake brushes for 40 years, from the time he began learning the trade from his father right after junior high school. He continued on through high school and college, where he studied chemistry. Today, he brings both his scientific knowledge and his mastery of traditional brushmaking methods to bear in creating new hake brushes.

小林刷毛制作所

千叶县习志野市藤崎5-7-5
0474-72-3431

Photo/高桥洋平

TOKYO BUTSUDAN
东京佛龛

东京佛龛最早可追溯至江户时代后期（1840年左右），始于江户做佛像的手艺人安田松庆制作的佛龛，其特点是，原料采用黑檀、紫檀、屋久杉等硬木，凸显木材本来所具有的天然木纹之美。

东京佛龛的制作工序大致可分为四步：原木加工、雕刻、上漆、组装。为了制作出坚固的成品，每道工序在技术上都要求严丝合缝。青嶋由雄制作的东京佛龛曾获得东京都知事奖等为数众多的奖项。

Butsudan craftsman Shokei Yasuda gave the traditional Buddhist family altar a signature look toward the end of the Edo Period, with techniques and materials unique to what is now the Tokyo area. The Tokyo butsudan is made from ebony, rosewood or Yakusugi cedar, specially crafted to bring out the natural beauty of the wood grain. Precision craftsmanship is a must in each of the many production processes, to ensure that the butsudan is hard and durable enough to be passed on from generation to generation.

 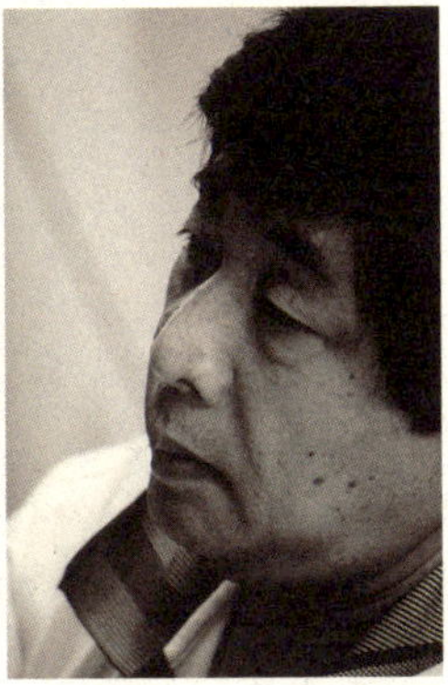

❖ 有限会社青嶋佛坛制作所

青嶋由雄

青嶋由雄先生幼年时便跟着父亲学做佛龛。他认为，“手艺人该做的就是按照吩咐埋头去做；要是怕麻烦，那就不要做手艺人”。他的切身感受是，“最重要的是与人的沟通”。工余时间他会热心地为街道居民会议统计出勤率，筹划孩子们的跳蚤市场。要是在外面做工，几乎每隔五分钟就会有街上的熟人和他打招呼。他生于斯长于斯，不忘匠人的天职，这样的手艺人向来有着好人缘。

One of the nation's premier butsudan makers, Yoshio Aoshima mastered the art when he was very small, helping his father create the altars. He has distinct views on his craft: "I suppose you can call me a craftsman, but I'm just a man who builds a place of prayer for people, as they want it built. It's simple work, really, but if I love it. And if I ever tired of it, I'd give it up." His work in creating Tokyo butsudan has been recognized with multiple Tokyo Metropolitan Government awards.

有限会社青嶋佛坛制作所

东京都台东区台东4-21-21
03-3831-8713
展示室：东京都台东区台东 3-27-7

Photo/星HIKARU

EDO TSUMAMI KANZASHI
江户花簪

用一把小钳子将一块薄薄的小绸布一捏一撮，一朵花簪就做成了。这种点缀在“七五三节”女孩头上，或身着和服的妇人秀发上的花簪，可以是四季不同的花花草草，也可以是各种小生灵。

表现温柔和美的“圆花”，表现坚强有力的“角花”，个性各异的花簪用途不一样，但都是靠着匠人灵巧的双手制作出来的。

江户花簪制作技艺历史悠久，其制作方法和表达意境的手法源自江户时代，是日本独有的一门手艺。目前，能制作江户花簪的匠人只有15人。

Tsumami Kanzashi are ornamental hairpins named for the pinching (tsumami) process by which they are created: fine squares of dyed silk are "pinched" with tweezers into the correct shape and placed onto adhesive backing. Most kanzashi adorn the coiffures of kimono-clad girls celebrating the shichi-go-san festival on the occasion of turning three, five or seven years old, and of grown single women in their formal furisode kimonos. Kanzashi handiwork is unique to Japan, with a proud history dating back to the Edo Period. However, only about 15 kanzashi makers remain to ply the craft today.

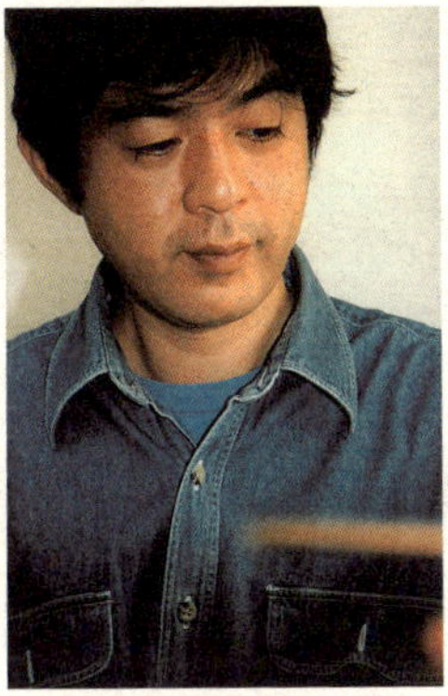

❖ 花簪博物馆

石田毅司

居住在新宿的石田毅司先生从父亲手上接下代代相传的花簪制作技艺，成为了一名匠人。花簪整个制作过程都由他一人完成。每当做成的花簪恰如其分地表达了人的思想，他便真切感受到了自己劳动的价值所在。他会不断想出新的造型，反复尝试，直到最后品尝到如愿以偿的喜悦。石田毅司先生并不止步于自我满足，为彰显江户花簪的社会价值，他还将制作完成的江户花簪送到百货店进行展示、销售。

Shinjuku craftsman Tsuyoshi Ishida took over tsumami kanzashi production from his father, and today handles all phases of the process himself. His attachment to the craft is quite emotional: nothing is more rewarding for an artisan than finishing a product that embodies his own passion while also expressing the passion of the wearer. His tsumami kanzashi are displayed and sold at department stores, among other venues.

花簪博物馆

@ www.ask.ne.jp/~kanzasi/

Photo/清水真纪子

TOKYO GAKUBUCHI
东京画框

手工制作的画框，早期主要用于寺院神社、佛堂建筑的屋顶或牌坊上，称之为“篆额”。按照画家的要求，先由木匠做成木框，再由做佛像的手艺人进行雕刻，最后由漆匠涂上油漆，这样才算大功告成。

到了明治时期，欧美文化影响日甚，西洋画（油画）的绘画技艺传到了日本，便开始出现了一揽子完成画框制作的手工作坊，当时的漆匠长尾健吉在芝爱宕町开设了一个小作坊，这被看作是“东京画框”制作的祖师。

Originally, gakubuchi were framed pictures created under the direction of the painting artist, with skilled joiners putting together the wooden frame, and busshi -sculptors of Buddhist statues-doing the woodcarving of the image, which was then lacquer finished by nushi artisans. However, studios capable of more unified frame production arose during the Meiji Period, with the introduction of techniques for western-style (yoga) oil painting. The first frame production center is believed to be the small factory built by Kenkichi Nagao at Shiba Atago-cho.

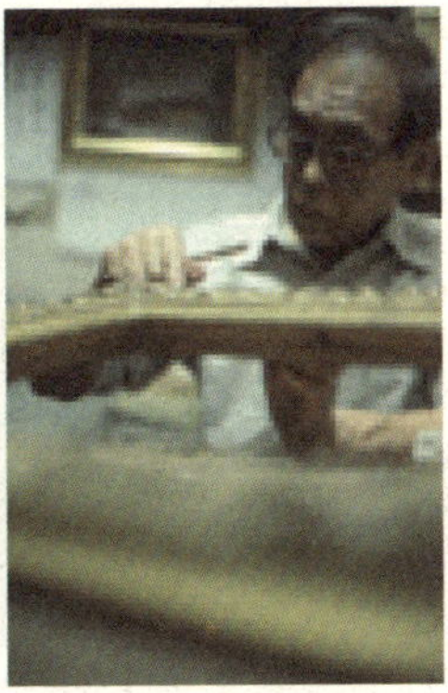

❖ 有限会社大江额缘店

大江洋一

从六本木十字路口步行十分钟，就到了大江额缘（画框）店，这家店开在六本木大街上已有好些年头。大江先生制作的画框最大的特点是厚重，有品位，装饰的图案尤其精美。“对我来说，没有做不了的画框。”大江先生笑呵呵地说，口气中充满了自信。如今虽然是使用现成的画框成了主流，但是每当有大型的画展临近，画家们还是会找大江先生度身定制画框。只要手工制作的需求还在，匠人之魂就不会消失。

The Oe Gakubuchi Frame Shop established its store on Roppongi Dori early in the history of modern frame production. Frames available there now, created by Yoichi Oe, acclaimed for his superb patterning technique, convey a stately dignity, their defining feature. Today the shop principally sells ready-made frames, but whenever a major art exhibition draws near, orders pour in from the exhibiting artists. The craftsman's spirit that informed the first gakubuchi frames remains alive and well in at least one Tokyo location.

有限会社大江额缘店

东京都港区六本木4丁目1-18
03-3403-3026

Photo/篝美也子

说起象牙，可能会让人联想到走私。
其实江户象牙所采用的原料来自于自然死亡的大象，或是为保持生态平衡，在政府管制下所取得的象牙。

EDO ZOGE
江户象牙

奈良时代传到日本的象牙制品，到了江户时代便广泛普及开来，出现了用象牙制作的坠子、梳子等日常生活用品。

如今，最常见的象牙制品是印章，这说明，从使用感觉上来说，用象牙制作的实用品有它的过人之处。目前，象牙主要从南非、津巴布韦、博茨瓦纳、纳米比亚等四个国家进口。在这些国家，大象得到保护，拥有的大象头数稳定在一定范围，象牙出口依据《华盛顿公约》进行。

Ivory work, or zoge, started in Japan during the Nara Period, reaching the height of its popularity during the Edo Period, when ivory combs and detailed miniature sculptures known as netsuke became everyday artifacts. Today, demand is greatest for use in personal seals, although supply is limited, since Japan has implemented an ivory control regime under the terms of the Washington Treaty restricting global trade in endangered species.

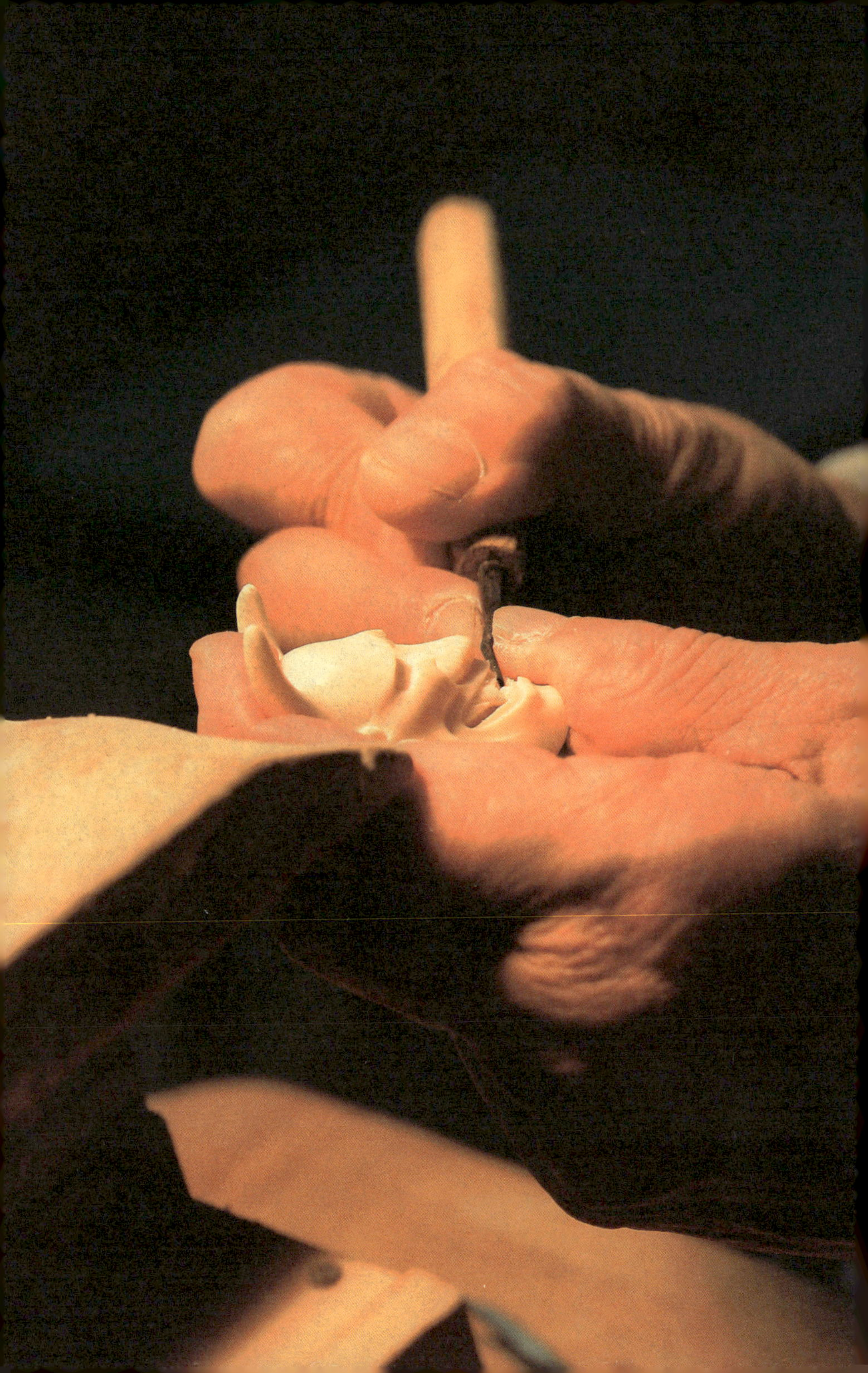

❖ 樱井牙雕制作所

樱井实

樱井实先生生于1935年，他是日本象牙美术工艺联合会会长、东京象牙美术工艺协会理事长。他15岁起就师从父亲樱井广晴学艺，60多年来，一直以象牙手艺人的身份潜心刻制，守护着这一传统手艺。他的兄弟也是象牙手艺人，他家堪称象牙世家，而樱井实本人则已带出了四位徒弟。如今，樱井实先生不单单是一位象牙手艺人，还是一位热心的协会干部，为保证有稳定的象牙来源作出努力。“象牙制品不单是一种实用品，它还有一定的工艺品价值。死去的大象化成作品后，可以永远留存下来。”

Minoru Sakurai mastered ivory work as a boy, under the tutelage of his father Hiroharu. In the ensuing 50 plus years, he has carved a niche for himself as an acclaimed ivory craftsman, a member of a prolific family of ivory workers. Sakurai is presently a trade association leader, devoted to maintaining a steady and sustainable supply of ivory to sustain the craft. "Once an elephant dies, it is incumbent on craftsmen to make sure it lives on in artistry," he says, touching on his greatest passion.

樱井牙雕制作所

东京都板桥区东新町 1-51-2
03-3955-1850

Photo/吉原克则

在作坊工作时，他又是一副绝然不同的表情。那认真不含糊的眼神似乎是要将生命注入木材中。

EDO SASHIMONO
江户木工艺品

这里所说的木工艺品，是指不用一只铁钉将板材组合起来，且接合之处隐藏不露的家具的总称，比如抽屉、梳妆台、置物箱等。这种木工艺品在日语中称为“指物”，大致可分为两类，一类是装饰豪华的“京式指物”，一类是突出质朴感的“江户指物”。

在外观上特意显露原木木纹肌理的“江户指物”，烘托出人们所追求的“自然风”，非常吸引眼球。

Sashimono is a type of furniture constructed only with (mortise and tenon) joinery, but no nails and screws. The interlocking is entirely internal, so that it cannot be seen on any outer surface of a finished piece. Drawers, mirror stands, trash receptacles and other interior items for Japanese rooms are created in the sashimono style. In Edo sashimono, different kinds of trees are used, carefully selected for their distinguishing characteristics, with the focus on maintaining the natural design of the wood in the finished piece. Thus, the eye-catching beauty is provided by nature and channeled though the craftsman.

这是对板材接合处进行加工时的情景，这种被称之为“接卯榫”的活，最能考验手艺人的技术水平。

NO.3303
KAMOI
EG
N25

林林总总的凿子，有平头的，也有圆头的，依照加工的需要选择使用。

❖ 大渊木艺

大渊浩吉

大渊浩吉先生是大渊浩藏的长子，出生在东京。他中学毕业后跟随父亲学艺，成为第二代传人，后来便搬迁到现在的住址。在大渊浩吉先生的木材仓库里，到处堆满各种木材。“我一见到好的原木就忍不住要出手，这给家人带来了不便，我内心充满了歉意。”现在，第三代传人、大渊浩吉先生的长子大渊光高已继承了这门手艺。“他才干了五年，以后的路长着哩。”说这话时，大渊浩吉先生的眼神既严厉又充满了喜悦之情。

Kokichi Obuchi was born in Tokyo, the eldest son of a sashimono artist. After graduating junior high school, he mastered the craft under his father's tutelage, eventually taking over the family furniture-making business. Always on the lookout for superior material, his workplace is crammed with mulberry, cypress and other wood waiting to be incorporated into traditional Japanese furniture. His eldest son Mitsutaka is being groomed to carry on the family tradition to the third generation.

大渊木艺

埼玉县川口市芝 4060-6

048-265-9106

Photo/丸山英树

EDO SUDARE
江户帘子

帘子非常实用。

帘子既通风，又遮阳，不停晃动的帘子似乎可以看见风的身影。轻便省事的帘子，集功能性和艺术性于一体，体现了日本式的智慧。

在制作上，江户帘子充分利用竹子、胡枝子、蒲草、芦苇等材料的纯天然本色，对色彩、大小尺寸、剪裁手法的选择等，每道工序都十分讲究，制作过程从古至今未曾改变。

Sudare, or matchstick blinds, are made of stems of bamboo, bush clover (hagi), birch (kaba), ditch reed (yoshi) and other natural materials, bound or plaited together in their natural state with cord. Spaces are left between them that allow air to pass through easily, while blocking out the light. The spare design of the sudare blinds is the embodiment of Japanese wisdom, highlighting functionality and artistry.

❖ 田中制帘所

田中耕太朗

父亲田中义弘是第四代传人，田中耕太朗是第五代传人，父子二人都是东京都传统工艺师。田中制帘所以他们父子俩为中心集聚了多位匠人制作帘子，是始于明治初期的江户帘子的老字号。在堆满了材料和工具的作坊间里，匠人们默默地劳作。第五代传人田中耕太朗更是一个彬彬有礼、待人真诚和气的人。

Tokyo's premiere Sudare producer is the Tanaka Sudare Workshop, where the forth-generation proprietor, Yoshihiro Tanaka, and his son and heir, Kotaro Tanaka, work silently among others. The workshop has continued in business since the beginning of the Meiji period. Both Yoshihiro and Kotaro Tanaka are Tokyo's premiere certified traditional craftsmen, who are eager in their work and have courteous and warmhearted personalities.

田中制帘所

东京都台东区千束 1-18-6
03-3873-4653

Photo/齐藤沙绫香

EDO SARASA
江户花布

花布发祥于3000多年前的印度，后来穿越大海，在室町至桃山时代传到日本。这种充满异国情调的染织品，从印度经由中国的丝绸之路传到日本，在漫长的历史中浸透了人们各种各样的浪漫思绪。

江户花布是在棉布上印上五彩缤纷的花样，色彩鲜艳，富有异国情调。所以，它不仅仅用于制作和服，还用来制作头巾和其他各种衣饰用品，令人耳目一新。

Sarasa dying originated in India, more than 3,000 years ago. It was introduced to Japan during the Muromachi Period, and spread further during the Momoyama Period. Sarasa dyed cotton is a riot of five colors that create exuberant and exotic patterns, reminiscent of batiks. The technique is widely employed for kimonos, but sarasa is also used to make colorful handkerchiefs, scarves and other accessories.

Y
R
P

❖ 染之里 二叶苑

小林元文

目前东京都内只有三间工坊在制作江户花布，其中一间便是“染之里二叶苑”。第四代传人小林元文说：“江户花布还有很多亟待我们去探索的地方。我很想把染织品的美丽、妙趣之处传承下去。”

Only three dye houses in Tokyo are still active in the sarasa silk-dyeing trade. One is the Some no Sato Futaba-en, run by fourth-generation kimono maker Motobumi Kobayashi. After all his time in the business, he remains stricken by what he calls the "incalculable charm" of sarasa. For Kobayashi, sharing his craft is his mission. "I want to pass the beauty and fascination of silk dyeing on into the future."

染之里 二叶苑

东京都新宿区上落合2-3-2
03-3368-8133

Photo/高木佳代

TOKYO HONZOME YUKATA
东京手染浴衣

浴衣本来是洗澡的时候裹在身上的衣物，其历史最早可追溯到平安时代。

到了江户时代，随着澡堂的普及，去公共浴池洗澡成为一种风俗习惯。那时，洗好澡，穿上一件印有中条花纹的棉质浴衣是一种时尚。直到进入明治时代以后，人们才渐渐地在赶集、祭日或赏烟花等热闹的节日穿着这种浴衣外出。

对浴衣、布手巾的需求在昭和三四十年代（1955-1965年）达到了顶峰，现在则是布手巾成了主力商品。“旭染工”每年要漂染10万“反”（布匹的长度单位，一“反”约宽34厘米，长10米—译者注）布料，一“反”布料可制11条手巾。

The yukata began to take shape in the Heian Period, when a wide-sleeved cotton kimono was worn to the bath. When public baths became common during the Edo Period, the modern unlined yukata-style kimono came in to vogue. The custom of wearing the yukata to festivals and events, or for casual strolls on summer evenings, took hold later, during the Meiji Period.

❖ 旭染工株式会社

阿部晴吉

阿部晴吉先生出生于1946年，今年已70岁了。早年因为父亲是漂染工场的老板，所以在18岁那年，他便从事手工漂染浴衣的工作。40岁左右，他接过了工场，如今还担任着关东注染工业协会的理事长。“旭染工”的非同寻常之处在于“资深匠人的技术力量”。阿部晴吉先生的信条是：“为满足顾客的多样化需求，把一切做到最好。”现在，“旭染工”已将产品打入地处日本桥的纺织品批发商户田屋、丸久商店等。

When Haruyoshi Abe was born in 1946, his father was running the kimono factory. Harukichi began making honzome yukata at age 18, and was in charge himself by around 40. Today he sits on the board of directors at the Kanto Dyeing & Weaving Industry Association. Speaking about his own facilities at Asahi Senko, he mentions "the technical expertise of our veteran craftsman" as the company's greatest advantage.

旭染工株式会社

东京都足立区花畑2-14-6

03-3883-0014

Photo/肥田木智子

TOKYO HONZOME YUKATA
东京手染浴衣

浴衣始于平安时代初期，是沐浴的时候裹在身上的单衣，称为“浴帷子”；到了江户时代中期，则是指刚洗好澡时所穿的衣服；直到明治时代，才变成现在这种夏天外出时穿的衣服。

东京手染浴衣是将以靛青为基调的染料充分印染在棉质的布料上，成为一种充满质感的棉质精品。其滑爽的肌肤触感、染布上荡漾着的清凉感和高品位的时尚感，绝非一般流行的机染浴衣可比。

The Tokyo Honzome yukata is created with indigo applied to cotton fiber in the traditional Japanese art of pattern dyeing. The dye is allowed to seep completely through the cloth, creating an exuberant interplay between color and texture, and a finished product of understated elegance and timeless beauty. Its soft touch and the chic, cool feel the dye gives off sets a true Tokyo honzome apart from the fleeting fashion of the print yukata.

❖ 有限会社村井染工场

村井米扶

村井米扶先生于1936年2月26日出生在东京，这天正是“二二六事件”发生的日子。他12岁就参与家庭生产，1957年5月，他作为第二代传人继承了家业。1990年2月被认定为东京都传统工艺师。现在较多的是生产各季的布手巾，订货的客户从企业、团体到单口相声演员、演歌歌手，范围十分广泛，据说已故演歌歌手美空云雀也十分爱用他们家生产的布手巾。这种认真专注、一丝不苟的手工制作慢慢地形成了一种精致的浴衣文化。今后，村井米扶先生将与第三代传人村井光寿一起，把这一文化传给后人。

Yonesuke Murai was born on the day 1,400 junior military officers launched an infamous uprising against the Japanese government, February 26, 1936. By the age of 12 he was working and learning the family business, which he eventually took over from his father in May 1957. Murai continues creating yukata with the skill, patience and painstaking attention to detail that define the true craftsman. Together with his son and heir Mitsutoshi, he is working to bring the beauty of traditional Japanese fabrics and the values of yukata culture to the wider world.

有限会社村井染工场

东京都江户川区一之江6-17-27

03-3651-3108

Photo/佐藤正崇

EDO WAZAO
江户和竿

江户和竿是指以天然竹子为材料上漆制成的可接可卸的钓竿，以17世纪后半叶，泰地屋东作在下谷稻町的广德寺前开设手工作坊为其起源。

江户和竿制作精致，它不单纯是一种钓具，更是一种玩赏性很高的雅趣物品，有的还在竿尾或卷线器上镶有玳瑁和象牙。从钓竿的式样到其他任何一个细节，制作和竿可根据客户要求“量身定制”，所以，你完全可以拥有一根世界上独一无二的江户和竿。

The Edo wazao is a special bamboo rod, made of whole, natural unsplit bamboo and lacquer finished, used as a traditional fishing rod. Tosaku Taichiya commercialized it in the late 17th century, developing what was a perfectly personalized product, from selection of the bamboo to the final finish. Because each wazao was built to individual taste and specification, no two ever created were exactly the same.

将干燥后的竹子放在火盆上烤热，矫正弯曲之处。
此时，要用一种叫作“矫木”的工具不停地修直原本欠挺直的竹子。这是向竹子注入灵魂的瞬间。

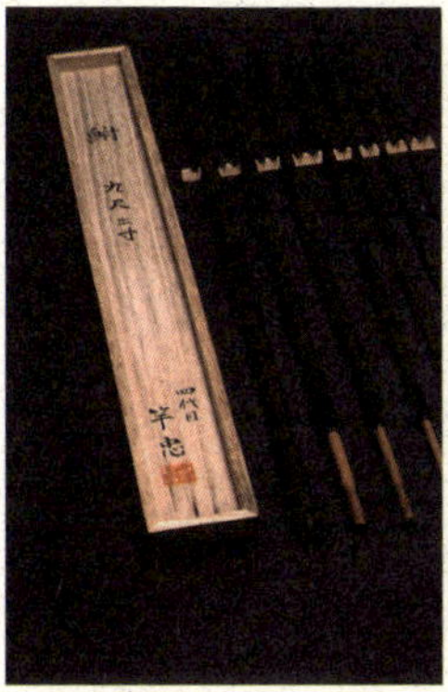

❖ 竿忠

中根喜三郎

中根喜三郎先生是“竿忠”的五世第四代传人，如今担任江户和竿协会的理事长。“竿忠”原先是家业单传给长子的，作为中根家族中第三个儿子，中根喜三郎本来并没有成为制竿师的打算。后来，他的父母和两个哥哥都在东京大空袭中丧生，生活窘迫的他在父亲中根音吉的好友三游亭金马的劝说下，决意继承家传手艺，成为一名制竿师。中根有家训曰：“不能做出连自己都接受不了的和竿，更绝对不能将这样的货色交给客户。”这就是匠人的精神。

As the great-grandson of the famous craftsman Saochu, Kisaburo Nakane is a fourth generation Edo wazao maker. He also serves as director of the Edo Wazao Cooperative Association. Originally, the family business was to be passed on to his brother, the eldest son, but the Nakane home was destroyed in the air raids of WWII, and Kisaburo lost his two older brothers. He then committed himself to becoming an accomplished wazao craftsman, with a drive and a faith in his art that has never diminished. "I could never allow myself to make wazao that I don't entirely believe in, much less deliver anything less than the very best to the customer."

竿忠

东京都荒川区南千住5-11-14
03-3803-1877

Photo/小林修一

EDO ISHOGININGYO
江户着装人偶

江户着装人偶最早可追溯至源氏物语的故事时代，到了德川纲吉时期才成为平民百姓的玩具普及开来。从种类上看，人偶既有身着艳丽服装的艺妓，也有稚气可爱的娃娃。其中尤以模仿歌舞伎演员"佐野川市松"姿势的人偶人气最为爆棚，这便是今日市松人偶的由来。

江户着装人偶采用天然材料制作，要经过上百道传统手工制作工序，它不可能大量生产，所以每件产品都独显其高贵典雅的风采。

Edo costume dolls (isho ningyo) arose from a tradition dating back to the days of the Genji Monogatari. Costume dolls had become popular during the reign of the Shogun Tsunayoshi Tokugawa in the late 17th century. In addition to baby dolls, the figurines represented courtesans and geisha dressed in the fashionable kimono of their time. These Japanese fashion dolls are made using techniques refined over the generations, for a timeless elegance that their mass-manufactured counterparts cannot hope to reproduce.

❖ 市松人形工房 松菊

菊地之夫

菊地之夫先生1957年出生在葛饰区，早年师从父亲菊地贞吉学艺，后来就一直专注于人偶制作。经过刻苦钻研，他不仅能制作市松人偶，还掌握了男童节人偶、女儿节人偶的制作方法。现在，菊地之夫先生正精益求精，用自己掌握的传统技艺制作天下最好、最受人们欢迎的人偶。

Yukio Kikuchi was born in Tokyo's Katsushika Ward in 1957. From the time he began studying under his father Sadakichi, his life has been devoted to doll-making. During a long formal apprenticeship, he mastered both the Ichimatsu play dolls that have captivated generations of Japanese children, and the exquisitely crafted hina ningyo representing the Imperial court. Kikuchi continues honing his skills, hoping to please his most demanding critic-himself.

市松人偶工房 松菊

东京都葛饰区青户3-41-3
03-3602-1452
www.ichimatsu.com

Photo/大竹邦昭

EDO KIRIKO
江户雕花玻璃

这种雕花玻璃工艺品在日语中称作“江户切子”。所谓切子，是指在玻璃容器的表面进行雕刻的技术，据说是在天保年间(1830~1844年)在江户普及开来的。到了明治以后，随着西方餐具、日用器具的引进，玻璃制品的工艺化制作受到刺激，变得更加大众化起来。

到后来，这个行业便在墨田、江东地区被当作本地产业获得发展，主要产品有钵盂、碟子、水杯、酒杯等。加工时，先在玻璃坯子上画好底样，然后用圆盘形砂石打磨，依样完成设计后进一步细磨，一件精美绝伦的江户雕花玻璃工艺品便诞生了。

通常采用的图案有：蛛网纹、龟甲纹、鱼子纹、编织纹、菊花等。

The exquisite cut glass craft known as kiriko gained popularity during the Edo Period, and developed as a local industry in the Sumida River area of Edo. Expert glassblowers and glasscutters create the ornate kiriko glassware, including bowls, dishes, glasses, and sake cups. After the glass is blown into a paper-thin, two-layer structure, the pattern design is cut into the glass using different kinds of whetstones, and the kiriko piece is then polished to a finish.

90° 150 30T 500M
90° 150 500M
90° 200 500M

❖ 有限会社根本硝子工艺

根本幸雄

获得过无数奖项的根本幸雄先生是一位具有代表性的玻璃工艺品制作大师，在创作过程中时常进行产品创新。战后，为了生存，他选择了这一行当。他儿子根本达也在年轻的时候为了养家就近入道学起了玻璃雕刻这门手艺，很早就掌握了雕刻技术，其技艺之精，在日本屈指可数。儿子在绘画、书法等美术方面也很有才华。在当地，底层的平民中间有很浓郁的子承父业的氛围。

Yukio Nemoto is virtually synonymous with Edo kiriko, having won numerous awards for his work in the glass medium. His son Tatsuya quickly mastered and incorporated glass sculpture techniques into his own kiriko work, making him one of the most technically gifted craftsmen in Japan. The tradition of superior kiriko craftsmanship continues unbroken to Nemoto's grandchild, blessed with the same sense of artistry.

有限会社根本硝子工艺

东京都江东区龟户8-9-4
03-3682-2757
www.fides.dti.ne.jp/~n-kiriko

photo/高桥稔

EDO OSHIE HAGOITA
江户贴画毽球板

用棉布包些棉花，然后在上面绘出各种各样的立体图案，这在日语中叫作“押绘”，将“押绘”贴在毽球板上，这门手艺始于江户时代初期。

到了江户时代后期，当绘有歌舞伎演员舞台造型的贴画毽球板一面世，立刻引得人气爆棚。由江户草根文化创造出来的工艺品江户贴画毽球板与歌舞伎艺术一同发展，其传统的制作手艺被传承到了今天。

在日本，自古就有新年时节向刚出生的女婴赠送毽球板的习俗，人们相信这样能够辟邪消灾。

There is a popular Japanese game -played for over 500 years- which resembles badminton but uses no net. It features a rectangular wood paddle (battledore), known as a hagoita, decorated with various images, sometimes executed in relief. At the beginning of the Edo Period, these patterns became more elaborate, with artisans creating intricate designs on the back of the paddles using quilted silk in a way that suggested three-dimensional figures. These included ukiyoe caricatures of popular kabuki actors, as the battledore became a reflection of Edo mass culture. Traditional Edo oshiehagoita handicraft remains in demand today. Just as they did in the Edo Period, parents give their little girls the decorative paddles at the New Year to ward off evil spirits for the entire year.

❖ 南川人偶店

南川行男

南川行男先生1929年出生在墨田区，他现在是东京岁之市毽球板商协会会长。从1945年起，南川行男先生就开始从事毽球板的制作，至今入行70余年，堪称大家。南川人偶店现在主要制作用于在每年12月17日至19日举行的浅草毽球板展销活动中销售的毽球板。在作坊里，南川行男先生从四周装饰得琳琅满目的毽球板中挑出一块男用毽球板，微笑着问："漂亮吗？"那神情同专注于制作毽球板时完全不同，透着匠人独有的温柔。

Yukio Minamikawa was born in Sumida Ward, Tokyo in 1929. He has been making hagoita for 70 years, ever since the end of the war. Although he produces a wide variety of the decorative paddles, his main focus is the lavishly decorated hagoita sold at the Asakusa Hagoita Fair, in the hope of an auspicious start to the New Year, from December 17 to 19 every year. Mr. Minamikawa is head of the Tokyo Sainoichi Hagoita Association.

南川人偶店

东京都葛饰区高砂3-7-11

03-3657-3975

Photo/细井由纪

EDO KACCHU
江户甲胄

江户甲胄是民俗节日装饰甲胄工艺师继承代代相传的古老制作技术和工艺，用手工制作的工艺品。在制作上，工艺师参考已被指定为国宝或重要文化遗产的古代甲胄，综合金属加工、油漆、编织、染色、皮革加工等多种工艺技术，完美再现古代甲胄的威仪。

精巧的制作手艺使得历史上曾经名震一时的武将穿戴的甲胄栩栩如生，也确立了江户甲胄独一无二的地位，其作为一件工艺品，具有极高的艺术欣赏价值。

Edo armor, or katchu, consists of elaborate festival garments and ornaments handmade by armor artisans. These are faithful reproductions of the armor worn by famous warlords in feudal times: individual, idiosyncratic, sometimes flashy statements of military class status. Today the unique armor creations are highly regarded works of art.

加藤鞆美

加藤鞆美先生是名匠、第一代加藤一胄的次子。日本全国各地的神社、佛寺至今仍保存着不少古代的“奉纳铠”（日本古代武士向神许愿或还愿时供奉在神社中的铠甲——译者注）、头盔，在逼真仿制这些甲胄的技术上，加藤鞆美先生获得很高的评价，被誉为当今首屈一指的大家。他对历史上各个时期的甲胄了如指掌，他地道的东京口音让听者着迷。他对自己的穿着也有着与众不同的执着，从1954年起，他就爱穿斜纹布裤子，皮带已换了两根，但皮带扣还是原先的，就是那种老式的开了两个孔的圆头铁质的带扣。“每次过机场的安检时都会被拦下来！”加藤鞆美先生爽朗的说话声中流露出一股匠人的潇洒劲儿。

Tomomi Kato is one of the nation's leading artisans, specializing in stunning recreations of feudal armor and helmets, as well as offertories for shrines and temples. He is consumed with his work, having now become quite an expert on the history of armor, and is often holding forth on the subject whenever he's not actually creating the suits of armor themselves. Kato is a captivating speaker, as much for his Edokko (native Tokyo) style as for the fascinating subject matter.

东京都文京区向丘二丁目 26-9
03-3823-4354

Photo/高桥稔

EDO KACCHU
江户甲胄

甲胄也就是盔甲，盔保护头，甲保护身子，都是古代打仗时用来护身的。江户时代中期以后，甲胄除了原先的护身作用外，渐渐被用作节日的装饰品。

端午节是一个传统节日，这个节日承载着人们祈愿男孩能长得勇敢健壮的期望。那个时候，人们就在端午节装饰一些模仿著名武将的盔甲制作的缩小版甲胄和武士人偶；而如今则主要是装饰诸如铠甲、头盔、弓、大刀、草笠形盔、鲤鱼旗、篝火等。

Yoroi and kabuto-the famous suits of feudal armor and samurai helmets-were of course the accoutrements of war. However, from the middle of the Edo Period onwards, families with boys have been displaying warrior dolls decked out in miniaturized versions of the armor and helmets. It is part of the Boy's Festival celebration, when parents encourage their young ones to grow strong and brave. Armor was originally produced and worn in sets, but today feudal armor, feudal helmets and bows are often displayed separately.

❖ 加藤一胄工房

加藤博

加藤家族包括亲戚在内，是甲胄制作工艺人才辈出的家族。先辈加藤一胄早年曾带着画师游走四方，自费进行甲胄研究。加藤博先生为自己取了一个一胄的雅号，以当代一胄之名专注于甲胄研究。他从用来装饰的缩小版甲胄着眼，尝试恢复真正甲胄的原貌。对戏剧舞台上或电视剧中作为道具使用的甲胄，他主要在演员穿戴易于活动上下功夫；对于广告摄影中表现的甲胄，则研究如何适当变形更富吸引力……当代的甲胄工艺师还真得有满脑子的新鲜点子，要会随机应变，应对各种订货要求。

The Kato name is synonymous with armor artistry in Japan. As head of an extended family of prolific armor artisans, Hiroshi Kato has adopted the nom de plume Itchu, reflecting his status as a true artist in armor. He spares no expense traversing the nation with a painter in tow, studying and acquiring original suits of feudal armor, which he painstakingly reproduces in miniature for display purposes. Meanwhile, his full-size creations are in demand from a wide variety of clients, including theaters and television studios.

加藤一胄工房

东京都文京区本乡6-2-7 香川大楼
03-3811-5042

Photo/高桥稔

TOKYO TOKOGEI
东京藤艺

藤属于棕榈科的热带植物，并不在日本生长。

热带气候炎热、潮湿，用生长在这种环境下的藤编制的工艺品不仅具有艺术价值，还有很好的实用功能。匠人们凭着一手烂熟于心的手艺，将粗细不同、秉性各异的藤条一根一根地或折或卷做成的藤艺制品，充分展露其特有的柔软温和的特性。说起传统工艺，人们往往会有代代相传、一成不变的印象，但小峰RATAN出产的藤艺制品却更注重考虑人的实用需求。

Wicker is made from rattan, a special climbing palm that only grows in tropical regions outside Japan. Because it is strong against heat and humidity, there is brisk demand for woven wicker as furniture, among many other practical applications. However, wickerwork handicraft from true masters is also valued as art.

❖ 小峰藤艺株式会社

小峰尚

小峰尚先生1932年出生在浅草，现在是东京都传统工艺师。小峰尚先生13岁那年为躲避空袭疏散至长野，于是跟着当藤艺匠人的叔叔学手艺。他的作品先后在第一、第二届东京藤工艺名品展上获得东京都知事奖。1991年，小峰尚先生荣获“黄绶褒章”。本着要让使用者直接感受藤艺制品的魅力这一理念，小峰尚先生每个月都要在全国各地举行产品展示活动。他说：“我很想制作出适合人们需要的藤工艺品，希望这些实用性强的藤艺制品能给老年人和残障人士的生活带来帮助。”匠人制作的每一件工艺品都饱含着如此的心意。

One of Tokyo's premiere certified traditional craftsmen, Sho Omine was born in Asakusa, Tokyo, in 1932. During the war he was evacuated to Nagano to escape the air raids, a quirk of fate that led him to his craft. Mastering wickerwork under the tutelage of his uncle, Omine went on to win numerous awards for his wicker creations. Today he travels the nation with the wicker items, attracting users and aficionados at an array of exhibitions.

小峰腾艺株式会社

东京都墨田区押上2-10-15

03-3623-0433

Photo/品田良子

TOKYO KIRITANSU
东京桐木衣柜

江户时代流传下来的传统和匠人高超的手艺，成就了带有美丽直木纹的桐木衣柜，东京桐木衣柜是其中的佼佼者。东京桐木衣柜选用国产优质桐木作为原料，最高档的会津桐木经天然干燥处理后保证了衣柜的质量。

桐木之所以受到人们的青睐，缘于它良好的调湿作用和耐火的性能。当遇到湿度较高的环境，它会阻隔潮湿空气；而在干燥的环境下又能保持良好的通气性。桐木遇水会发生膨胀，阻断烟火，因而它又有阻燃的特性。

桐木衣柜用久了，还能进行翻新，翻新后就像新家具一样，所以它能伴随你一生。

Craftsmen use highly textured, straight-grain wood from the kiri, or paulownia tree, to create striking traditional Japanese chests. Tokyo paulownia chests incorporate the beautiful grain and superb luster of naturally dried Aizu paulownia-the finest in Japan. The unique structure of paulownia wood minimizes humidity and mildew to protect the chest's contents, while the structural quality of the wood makes it naturally fire resistant. Because they are meticulously cared for and can be restored as necessary, paulownia chests last a lifetime.

刨削木板，即使是薄如一张纸的误差也不放过。

❖ 合资会社林氏衣柜店

林正次

林正次先生是传统工艺师，东京都优秀技能者。1955年，他作为家业的继承者，跟随父亲学手艺。无论是对制作用材，还是作为匠人对手艺水平的追求，他都有着非同寻常的执着。比如对入手困难的桐木木材，只要听说哪里能得到优质木材，哪管天涯海角，他都会锲而不舍地去弄来。又比如对抽屉的制作，他又会用上自己的独门秘笈“燕尾榫”。国立历史民俗博物馆、东京江户博物馆存放历史资料的大型储存柜都是他精湛手艺的结晶。现在，林正次先生正将自己对技艺的执着传给林氏家业的第三代传人、他的儿子林英知。“我要干它一辈子！”这位浑身充满活力、老当益壮的匠人如此说道。

Masatsugu Hayashi is a superb traditional craftsman, and a recipient of the prestigious Tokyo Master designation. He was raised in the family chest- and cabinet-making business, trained in the craft under the direction of his father. Mr. Hayashi developed a very discerning eye for the materials he uses-every bit as important as his skills as an artisan. His work has also made him an accidental traveler of sorts: whenever hard-to-find paulownia comes onto the market, he must be ready to go get it, wherever it may be.

合资会社林氏衣柜店

东京都品川区二叶2-22-6
03-3782-1821

Photo/中山雅照

“江户刺绣”与众不同的地方在于创作的时候，在估量用线的粗细、绞线的松紧的同时，融入自己的捻线技巧。

EDO SHISHU
江户刺绣

飞鸟时代佛教传到日本后，开始出现用刺绣制作的佛像，即佛教绣像，这便是日本最早的刺绣品。

到了平安时代，因为有了朝臣贵族阶层，刺绣又成了点缀宫廷妇女礼服的装饰手段，互相竞逐的是奢靡豪华。

进入安土桃山时代后，刺绣增加了“着色”“收拢”等其他行业匠人的技术。而到了天下太平的江户时代，绚烂豪华的和服层出不穷，京式、加贺式、江户式等不同地方特色的刺绣品各竞所长、各有千秋。随着江户的繁荣，“江户刺绣”也应运而生并日渐发达。1987年，“江户刺绣”被认定为传统工艺品，在今日匠人的手中发扬光大。

Shishu embroidery in Japan began with the introduction of Buddhism and the importation of embroidered Buddha images in the Asuka Period. Japan's history can be seen in its shishu embroidery-incorporated in the junihitoe, or 12-layer unlined kimono worn by the noblewomen of the Heian Period, and the magnificently embroidered kimonos that appeared during the Edo Period.

在丈夫染制的“市松花纹”（方格）布料上设计好图案，然后一针一线地进行刺绣。

将从名为“釜丝”的桑蚕中获得的丝线捻合后用于刺绣。

江上工房内的工作情景。远处是手绘友禅传统工艺师江上昌幸在工作。

❖ 江上工房

江上芳子

江上芳子女士1943年出生在东京，2002年被认定为东京都传统工艺师。有许多刺绣匠人都是先请图案设计师绘好图样，或在友禅绸（一种印上花鸟、花卉等的丝绸——译者注）上进行刺绣，而江上女士则是亲自在和服、腰带、小件用品上绘上图样，然后进行刺绣，所以她的作品都是原创的。江上女士还常和丈夫、手绘友禅传统工艺师（国家级）江上昌幸先生联手创作作品，这样，江上工房便不断有让人惊艳的印染、刺绣作品问世。

Born in Tokyo, Yoshiko Egami was certified as a traditional artisan by the Tokyo Metropolitan government in 2002, for her design and embroidery of kimono, obi, and accessories (komono). While all her work is original design, she is famous for her many collaborations with friend and yuzen (printed silk) master Masahiko, herself certified as a traditional artisan by the government of Japan. Their works are an exuberant marriage of the nation's best embroidery and dyeing artistry.

江上工房

东京都练马区土支田2-30-18
03-3921-1207
egamikobo.fc2web.com

Photo/佐藤纯子

園田神佛具店
ダルマ
お買上げの方
御引取致します

EDO MOKUCHOKOKU
江户木雕

木雕的历史很久远，据传始于6世纪佛教传入日本之际。

从平安时代到镰仓时代，人们雕刻了很多佛像，后来到了不需要佛像的禅宗迎来全盛期的时候，专业从事神社寺庙立柱、格窗装饰的建筑雕刻业便迅速发展起来。建筑雕刻本来是木匠干的活，但到了江户时代，木匠师傅中分离出了专门从事装饰的“宫雕师”。

如今，江户木雕工艺师继承历史传统，主要从事装饰品、葬祭用具，以及建筑上的雕刻等。

Woodcarving has a proud history, dating back to the arrival of Buddhism in Japan. Originally, carpenters did all the architectural woodcarving in the nation's shrines and temples. However, as the art advanced and became more elaborate during the Edo Period, woodcarving work was taken over by miyaborishi, specialists in the art of woodcarving decoration. Edo woodcarvers continue this tradition, keeping alive the carving techniques handed down over the generations.

❖ 园田神佛具店

园田秀夫

1941年，园田秀夫先生出生在葛饰区柴又的一个开设神、佛像雕刻店的家庭里。他从小就在四周满是佛像的环境中长大，跟着父亲学习木雕手艺，随后接下了园田家族雕刻师的招牌“园田正信”，现在作为第三代传人正将木雕手艺发扬光大。如今，人们一走出柴又车站就能看见木雕匠人园田先生制作的木雕导览图。帝释天的入口处便是创建于明治时期的“园田神佛具店”，而相邻的民间工艺品商店也借着势头，销售“弹猴”之类当地的乡土玩具。

Hideo Sonoda was born in Shibamata, Katsushika Ward, Tokyo in 1941. Like many families in this enclave in the capital, the Sonodas were plying a traditional trade, running a shop specializing in Shinto and Buddhist woodcarving. Hideo grew up surrounded by Buddhist statuary. He trained in the woodcarving arts under his father, eventually attaining the level of artistry to assume the name Masanobu from the senior Sonoda and pass on the family tradition. Today the third-generation woodcarver looks back at his work with pride and forward with anticipation.

园田神佛具店

东京都葛饰区柴又7-6-14

03-3657-5997

Photo/ichi

TOKYO CHOKIN
东京雕金

雕金这门手艺也有很长的历史了，最早始于装饰刀剑、刀剑护手等金属零件的打造。

雕刻时要依照作品的用途，使用各种钢凿，以多种角度，如斜着凿、立着凿等，在金、银、白金、铜等不同金属底坯上进行雕凿。就技法而言，有细雕、蹴雕、镶嵌、深雕、浅雕、锄雕、镂花等。

1876年（明治9年）日本全面实施废刀令，“七七禁令”（指1940年7月7日实施的“关于限制奢侈品等生产销售的规定”—译者注）中又提出禁止使用稀贵金属的规定，时代在不断地变化，而雕金这门手艺如今也转换为制作珠宝饰品。

Japanese-style metalwork, or chokin, arose from the military tradition, beginning with decorative hand guards, scabbards and other sword accoutrement. Early metalworkers developed an array of chisels and other tools, each designed to create a different class of product or application. Adjusting the positions of the implements enabled metalworking craftsmen to grind, chisel and file to a fine finish gold, silver, platinum and copper. Most chokin specialists today are producing jewelry.

桌子上摆满了自制的用途各异的凿子。

手持凿子，精准錾刻。

❖ 清水雕金工房

清水洪政

清水洪政先生是东京都传统工艺技术保存联合会丰岛地区会员，1936年出生在福岛县，1947年师从雕金家柿岛义香学手艺，1950年创建清水雕金工房。现在是日本雕金会委员、审查委员，JCC会员，东京都传统工艺师，丰岛区传统工艺师，别号“香政”。被认定为传统工艺师之后，清水洪政先生每天埋头于文献资料，研究雕金的起源和流派。

Kosei Shimizu was born in Fukushima prefecture in 1936, and, while still an 11 year-old child, began to study under metalworking master Giko Kakishima. By 1950, he already had a hand in establishing the Shimizu Metalworking Craft Center. He is a member of the Judging Committee of the Nihon Chokin Kai, and sits on another of the nation's key metalworking organizations, the J.C.C. Mr. Shimuzu is officially recognized as a traditional craftsman of Tokyo, and of the Toshima Ward. He has taken the master's name Kasei.

清水雕金工房

东京都丰岛区驹込 7-10-9

03-3917-9487

Photo/纐缬哲广

TOKYO UCHIHAMONO
东京刀具

早在1500年前，冶炼技术就已传到了日本。

后来，这一技术到了制作刀剑的匠人手中被不断精益求精，没多久他们就发明了“着钢法”，即在用质地较柔软的铁锻造的刀刃上接上坚硬的钢，由此诞生了刀身虽软、刀刃却十分锋利的日本独有的刀剑。

进入太平盛世的江户时代后，原先打造刀剑的匠人开始转向民用，从事锻冶日常生活中使用的刀具的街头打铁作坊越来越多，打造刀剑的技术转而用在了制作产业用刀具、家用刀具上面。

Blacksmithing was introduced to Japan some 1,500 years ago, and was advanced technically and artistically by sword craftsmen, who forged uniquely Japanese, soft, sharp blades. These techniques were then further perfected by artisans working to develop blades for everyday civilian uses in the Edo Period.

锻打工序十分重要，铁锤敲下时不能有偏斜，哪怕是一点跳动都会留下伤痕。

❖ 正次郎铗刃物工艺

石塚洋一郎

54年前，石塚洋一郎先生的父辈就在千叶县成田机场附近建起了作坊，他出生在一个从江户时代后期起就一直从事锻冶的刀剑制作世家。19年前，他作为第五代传人继承了家业，并将作坊改名为“正次郎铗刃物工艺”。石塚洋一郎先生执着于一种名为“总火造”的技法，即刀具的刀刃和刀柄都要在火中锻打的制作手法。他坚信“货好不怕没人识”，精心制作出各种万能刀和烹饪小刀。

Yoichiro Ishizuka was born into a family of sword- and cutlery-makers with a pedigree stretching back to the late Edo Period. He established his own workshop near Narita Airport in Chiba Prefecture, where he has been producing fine cutlery for the last 54 years. Later, he assumed the title of Shojiro Hasami Hamono Kogei, becoming the fifth-generation master of the sword- and blade-making arts. Although Mr. Ishizuka primarily produces all-purpose kitchen knives and smaller cutlery, his craftsmanship remains true to the proud techniques that date back to the feudal swordmasters.

正次郎铗刃物工艺

千叶县成田市松崎697
0476-26-8061
www.shojiro.com

Photo/泉三郎

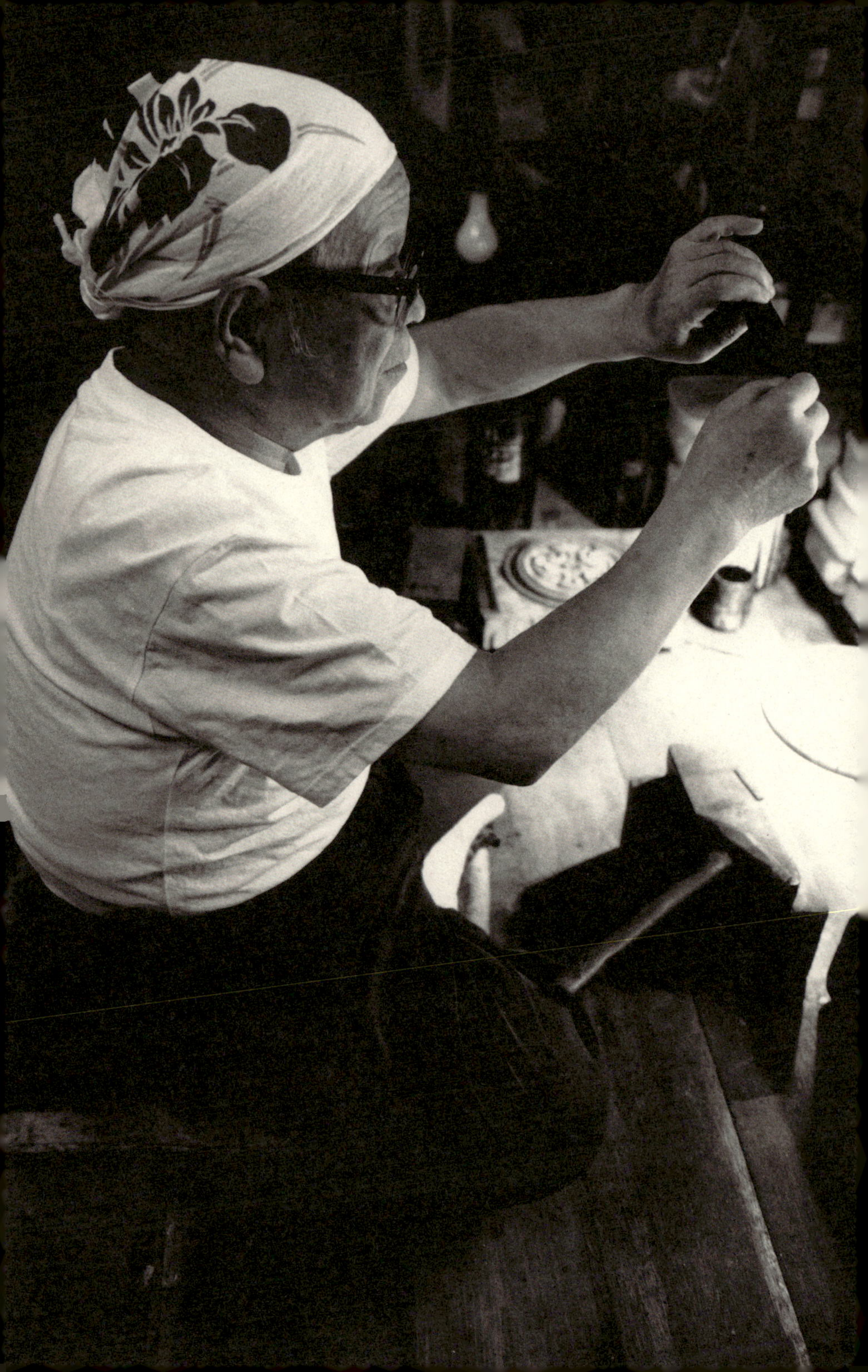

TOKYO UCHIHAMONO
东京刀具

明治初期，江户改称东京。从前以锻造刀剑为业的锻冶匠人，随着废刀令的实施和文明开化的发展，渐渐将产品制作的重点转向产业用或家用的刀具。

仅靠一把铁锤便将一条熟铁打造成一把刀，用的是日本刀的制作技艺，刀刃是否锋利决定了这把刀的质量。被誉为刀刃质量最好的东京刀具，多年来一直是众多匠人、厨师爱用的刀具。

Few in Japan were more profoundly impacted by the radical changes of the Meiji Restoration than sword-makers. With the decree banning the wearing of swords in 1876, these craftsmen had to switch to industrial and household forged blade production. However, subsequent generations of craftsmen continued applying the techniques of the sword-making masters to create some of the world's highest quality forged blades. Today, cooks and homemakers are among the beneficiaries of Japan's feudal sword-making tradition.

❖ 和弘利器株式会社

大河原辰雄/大河原享幸

大河原辰雄、大河原享幸兄弟俩将古老的锻造技艺“总火造”传承至今。他俩15岁便开始入行，已连续干了70年。这对兄弟配合默契一起工作的事迹为众多媒体所报道。他俩还经常到全国各地进行现场表演，向当今时代的人们展示刀具的魅力。“菜刀靠力气就能打造出来，但剪子光靠力气和经验是不行的，还需要懂造型才行。”如今，在东京的金町，锻造刀具的锤子敲打声仍不绝于耳。

The Okawara brothers, Tatsuo and Takayuki, remain true to Japan's traditional sobizukuri blade forging methods. Since becoming apprentices at the age of 15, the two have been making forged blades for 70 years, developing the chemistry that is obvious to anyone watching them work together today. They demonstrate their craft at exhibitions across the country, working to share the appeal of the blade-making arts.

和弘利器株式会社

东京都葛饰区金町1-10-8
03-3607-0833

Photo/笠原好美

在书画原作的背面反复裱上衬纸以制成可保存较长时间的结实的挂轴，这是一个考验技术水平的手工活。

EDO HYOGU
江户裱褙

裱褙，就是用纸或丝织品做衬托，做成卷轴、挂轴、书画帖、屏风、隔扇等，又称作装裱、装潢。裱褙历史悠远，在日本已有千年之久。历史上各个时期，不管是有名的还是无名的裱褙师，他们经受时代的洗礼，坚守匠心，使得这门手艺得以传承至今。

1989年，东京都将江户裱褙指定为传统工艺品，裱褙手艺人也不断下功夫创新，力图为这门古老的手艺注入新的技术，使之焕发新的生命。

Scrolls take many forms in Japan, including kakemono hanging paper or cloth scrolls, scrolls of calligraphy, folding screens and the paper coverings for sliding fusuma doors. In addition, paintings and calligraphy are finished as scrolls in a mounting process known as hyoso or hyoko in Japanese. After 1,000 years of artistic history, the scroll-making was certified as a traditional craft in 1989. Today, artisans continue building on the tradition, creating innovative new styles of scroll art.

浆糊是稠还是稀，要根据当天的天气、温度、湿度作出调整，这全凭匠人多年练就的直觉。

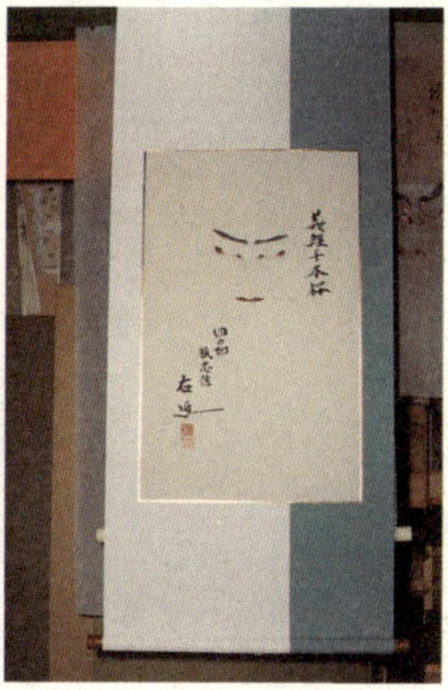

❖ 裱褙师前川

前川八十治

前川八十治先生作为父辈前川弥太郎的接班人，从事裱褙业至今已长达50多年，始终兢兢业业。1992年，获得“墨田区注册非物质文化遗产”的认定。他经手的众多裱褙作品中，以歌舞伎脸谱的装裱最有特色，可称得上是前川匠人的代名词。“我十分看重并珍惜同客户的缘分，”前川先生说，“对于裱褙师来说，对艺术的敏感和辨别力与技术同样重要。”所以直到现在，前川先生仍孜孜不倦地提高自己的手艺水平。

Yasoji Maekawa succeeded his father and mentor Yataro, becoming a scroll artist more than 50 years ago. After decades of superb work, he was recognized by Sumida Ward, Tokyo in 1992, when his skills were declared an intangible cultural asset. He is perhaps best known for his kumadori scrolls of kabuki faces.

裱褙师前川

东京都墨田区千岁3-5-11

03-3631-0508

Photo/山田宏次郎

用木栓、绳子、锲子等工具将蒙在共鸣箱上的皮绷到最紧，但又要防止绷破。

TOKYO SHAMISEN
东京三味线

追溯三味线的源头，那是从中国传到琉球的三弦琴。

后来到了室町时代末期，又从琉球传入泉州堺(今大阪府西南部)。此琴用拨子演奏，共鸣箱蒙有猫皮。到了江户时代，清元小调、长歌日渐流行，江户地区制作三味线也就兴盛起来。一把三味线大致由卷弦的弦轴、琴柄、蒙皮的共鸣箱三部分组成。在三味线的制作过程中，蒙皮这道工序分外重要，需要有熟练的技术，因为它决定了琴的音质。

The shamisen originated in China, and was introduced to Japan in its original three-stringed form through the Ryukyu Islands. The strings are wrapped around a pegbox (itogura), close to the fingerboard, which is of one piece with the neck. The soundbox is covered with animal skin, typically dogskin, catskin or snakeskin. A shamisen's sound quality is determined by the way this skin is attached to the soundbox, a process that requires exacting technical skill.

東京三味線 東京琴

进行最后的细微调整时用手指轻轻叩击皮的表面，从发出的声音和手指的触感确认绷紧的程度。“全凭感觉。”这是野口先生对这个活儿的体会。

❖ 菊音邦乐器店

野口哲彦

虽说父亲也是制作三味线的匠人，但野口哲彦先生一度曾在外谋职，只是后来因为“不习惯受人使唤”，最终才选择走上了匠人之路。现在，虽然三味线制作出现了细分化的趋势，但野口哲彦先生却是能一人熟练完成所有工序的少数几位匠人之一。三味线的制作中最需要用心的是蒙皮这件活儿，据说得看天气行事，下雨天是不能做的。具有匠人气质的野口哲彦先生还热心于日本古典音乐的普及工作，常到当地初中辅导学生演奏古乐。他虽已年逾古稀，却依然精神矍铄。

Tetsuhiko Noguchi's father is a shamisen artisan. Noguchi himself originally worked as a regular company employee, but was eventually drawn to follow his father on the path of shamisen craftsmanship. At the time, shamisen production had become specialized, with different craftsmen handling different parts of the process. Noguchi became one of very few artisans capable of creating a shamisen entirely by himself. In addition to his making the instruments, he teaches Japanese music at a local school, working in both capacities to keep the music of Japan thriving.

菊音邦乐器店

东京都文京区千駄木5-38-1

03-3821-2806

www.h4.dion.ne.jp/~kikuoto/

Photo/酒井裕司

“扎尾”：先用麻线将笔毫的根部扎住，然后用烧热的烙铁烫一下，趁热将麻线扎紧。

EDO FUDE
江户毛笔

江户时代中期，随着工商业的发达，“私塾”的数量也急剧增加，毛笔开始在平民百姓中普及开来。与此同时，江户制笔匠人的技术发展很快，诞生了许多江户名笔。

相对于关西地区制作的“固笔”（笔毫用胶水固定住——译者注），江户地区制作的大多是“捌笔”（笔毫不用胶水固定，而是散开的——译者注），不管粗笔还是细笔，笔毫虽然散开，笔尖却仍锋利，无论何时都能写出很细的线条。

Writing and drawing were relatively esoteric skills until the mid-Edo Period, when terakoya schools were established to provide education to commoners. Just at the point average citizens began using writing brushes, Edo craftsmen were improving their brush-making techniques. The watershed event in the development of the Edo writing brush was the creation of the sabakifude, a brush without a core and no starch applied to the head. Sabakifude brushes-large and small-collect at the tip to enable the user to write consistently fine lines.

“甄选”：依靠眼力和手感，鉴别制笔用毛的长短、毛尖的优劣，依照不同的用途进行区分。

“整毫”：将已成型的制笔用毛分成五至六部分进行整理，做到全部一样。

“分长短”：按需要将不同长度的制笔用毛分成几类。

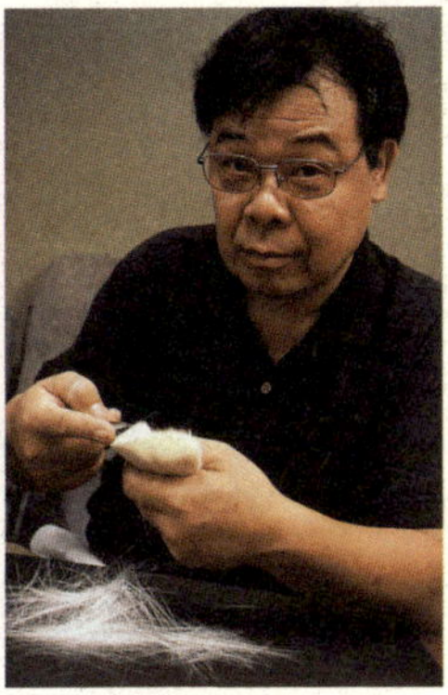

❖ 笔工房亀井

亀井正文

亀井家族的制笔业始于1877年，亀井正文先生继承了家传的技术、手艺，成了第四代传人。他家制作的毛笔多达850种，都是迎合书法家用笔的需要，结合自身的制笔技术制作的。他家出产的毛笔爱惜使用的话可用上二三十年，所以，亀井正文先生也接修损坏的毛笔。他说不管是制笔还是修笔，都是自己喜欢做的事。儿子亀井晓央才27岁，要成为经验丰富的制笔匠人至少还要干上六七年，亀井正文先生说，这个日子有点遥远。

Masafumi Kamei is the fourth in a line of writing brush artisans, inheriting techniques going back to 1877. He produces about 850 different types of writing brushes, each geared to the needs and skills of the individual calligraphers for whom they are made. Kamei writing brushes can be repaired, and owners of a Kamei take meticulous care of it. Thus, it is common for a brush to be used for 20, even 30 years.

笔工房亀井

东京都练马区石神井町5-14-2
03-3996-5046
www016.upp.so-net.ne.jp/fudeya/

Photo/斋藤真理

将刚染好的布料挂在竹竿上晾干。

TOKYO MUJIZOME
东京素染

和服是日本的传统民族服装，其中最基本的染色方式就是素染。

素染是按照客户提出的衣色要求，对制衣的布料进行单件染色；而且，因为是素染，经得起改染也是它的一大特点。

素染的工序大致可分为检查来料、过水、染色、对色、水洗、晾干、整理和检验等，很多都是手工作业，匠人熟练的手艺必不可少。

The kimono is one of the nation's most celebrated symbols, Japan's traditional costume. At its heart, the kimono is a triumph of dyeing technique. In patternless dyeing, each piece of fabric is dyed separately, to the specification of the order. Because it is patternless, the dye can be changed in mid-process, a defining feature that adds freedom and flexibility to kimono design. Kimono dyeing is largely performed by hand, an exacting process that demands the finely honed skills of experienced craftsmen.

上图／已加工完毕的布料经检验合格后被仔细卷成一捆捆，等待送往批发店。
下图／“绷手”（将染好的布料晾干时使用的工具）

上图／用熨烫机整理布料的长度和宽度。
下图／用专门的工具绷直布料，消除皱褶。

羽尺
コート

左图：有不少单口相声演员爱穿东京素染的和服。这是单口相声演员立川谈四楼，他身上穿的是“中央染工”印染的带有家徽的和服。

❖ 中央染工

大坪俊男/高须保/铃木信子

已有上百年历史的“中央染工”，第一代创业者在京都打下基业，后来利用在东京建立分部的契机，又迁到了东京。现在，已是第四代传人的西岛社长和夫人，同其他三位拥有40多年行业经验的资深匠人一起经营作坊，默默地坚守着这一传统文化。

The Chuo Dyehouse was founded 100 years ago in Kyoto. Fourth-generation dyemaster Toshio Otsubo relocated to Tokyo when the family established a kimono factory in the capital. Today, Mr. Otsubo is working with his wife and three veteran artisans-each with more than four decades of experience-to keep the traditional kimono arts thriving.

中央染工

东京都中野区本町6-27-17

03-3382-4116

Photo/井上雅惠

山本敬治先生设计的“梦想晕”。

TOKYO MUJIZOME
东京素染

素染（浸染）是最基本的染色法，历史悠久。这种染色法是将布料浸在用草木熬成的汁液里上色，所以也叫草木染。

随着佛教传入日本，被当作染色原料的蓼蓝、红花也接踵而来，同时也确立了染色的技术。到了镰仓时代，媒染剂发展很快；到了江户时代，“江户紫”成了歌舞伎名角团十朗扮演助六爱用的裹头巾，由此在民间广泛流行。

进入当代，科学技术发展后化学染料得到应用，而素染这一独特的染色法能将一袭和服的布料反复染上好几次，经常有母亲将这样的和服传给女儿继承。

Patternless dyeing is derived from the most fundamental and ancient method of coloring fabric-boiling out the natural dyestuff from plants and soaking the cloth in the extruded dye. More sophisticated dyeing technology and the use of indigo blue and safflower red came to Japan with the arrival of Buddhism. However, as modern science and technology developed further, natural plant dyeing techniques began giving way to the chemical processes that predominate today.

盛有各种染料的染缸。

同染好的布料进行对色。

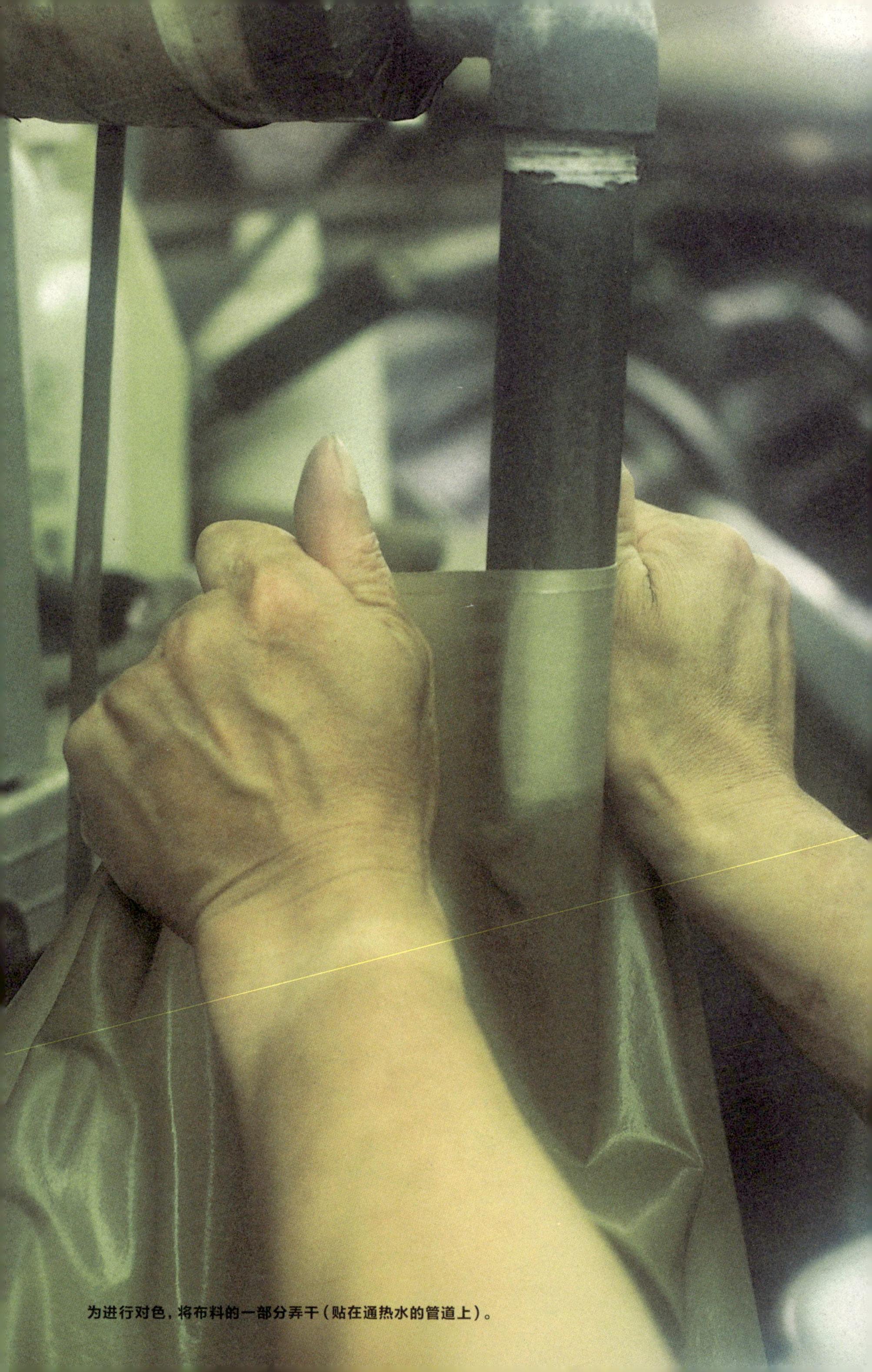

为进行对色，将布料的一部分弄干（贴在通热水的管道上）。

❖ 山本染工房

山本敬治

专注于素染技艺已有55年之久的山本敬治先生，在20多年前设计出一种名为“梦想晕”的色彩。当时，他用自己制作的器械印染布料，为了得到理想的浓淡度，花了三天到近一个星期的时间不断地调整布料的染色部分和染液的颜色，最后终于如愿以偿。取名“梦想晕”的意思是说，在山本先生将自己梦中想象的色彩变为现实之前，那只是他“在梦里见到过”的色彩。目前，浜田山的作坊是他和弟弟山本丰美一起经营的。

Keiji Yamamoto has been plying the art and craft of patternless dyeing for some 55 years. A little more than 20 years ago he conceived the musoun dyeing method for a more sophisticated, nuanced coloration. It involves setting the cloth up on a special device he designed himself, and applying a meticulous and time-consuming dyeing technique, designed to produce beautiful color gradations. His subtle but striking creations are the centerpiece of the traditional Japanese clothing factory that Yamamoto runs, along with his brother Toyomi.

山本染工房

东京都杉并区高井户东4-26-1
03-3332-1134

Photo/铃木贵美子

TOKYO KOTO
东京琴

东京琴最早是在江户时代晚期，由“山田流”的创始人山田检校改良制作的。东京琴长为六尺，琴身比通常的古琴短而厚，纵向弯度大，因而发声响亮。

另外，弹琴用的假指甲也做得大，音质显得特别明亮。制作琴身的材料一般是桐木、红木、紫檀木等，琴弦则使用丝线。

日本的古琴有山田流、生田流之分，唯有东京琴不问流派，受到人们的广泛喜爱。

The first Tokyo koto was created by Kenko Yamada, the founder of the Yamada school, an alternative approach to koto performance in the late Edo Period. The Tokyo koto is slightly shorter than its traditional predecessor, measuring six shaku, or about 1.8 meters, whereas the original koto is closer to two meters long. In addition, the Tokyo version is thicker, and distinguished by a more robust, clearer sound. It is made from materials including paulownia, ruby wood and red sandalwood, with silk threads used for the strings.

象牙曲物
紅木曲物見切材料
080-5512-2

❖ 金子琴三弦乐器店

金子诚次

金子诚次先生是日本少数几位能做到从原木直到成品都由一人独立完成的制琴匠人之一。从业80年来，他始终坚持琴身非用桐木（会津桐）制作不可，其制作的东京琴音质扣人心弦，令人难忘。从金子诚次先生对琴的叙述中，我们可以真切感受到这位老人将自己一生奉献给制琴业之后所具有的自信和尊严，以及对古琴倾注的深厚感情。

Seiji Kaneko is one of the few artisans in Japan capable of creating a koto from the hollowed out trunk of a paulownia tree without assistance in any of the processes involved. He has been carefully selecting paulownia for 80 years, turning the wood into vibrant yet reflective music that leaves an indelible impression on the listener.

金子琴三弦乐器店

东京都大田区千鸟3-18-3
03-3759-0557
www.kanekogakki.com

Photo/近藤和寿

在“浮线蝶”花样的木版上用筛子涂上一层浆糊。这个木版是幸雄先生自己翻刻的。

EDO KARAKAMI
江户花纸

制作江户花纸的匠人，按在纸面上添加装饰的不同技法分为“唐纸师”“砂子师”“更纱师”三种。其中“唐纸师”主要是以“木版手工印刷”为主，即先将一种名为“云母”的颜料涂在木版上，然后再放上日本纸拓印出花纹，这被认为是最古老的印制花纸的技法。

江户花纸用途广泛，隔扇、屏风、壁纸等都会用上它，如今在日本建筑的室内装饰中也少不了它的身影。

Edo karakami artisans produce three main varieties of decorative paper: karakamishi, sunagoshi and sarasashi. There are a variety of methods for creating the signature decorative patterns; which one is chosen depends on the type of paper to be made, and its application. Since the Edo Period, karakami has been employed for a wide variety of uses, including fusuma - sliding doors constructed of wooden frames and covered with layers of thick paper - and byobu folding screens. It is an essential part of Japanese interior design and construction.

在已涂上浆糊的花样上敷上金银箔，干燥后细磨一下让花纹浮现出来，这种手法叫“贴箔”。

在“萩”花样的木版上用筛子涂上“云母”，
然后再覆上日本纸，在纸上拓印出花样来。

“春举松”花样的壁纸（鹤冈八幡宫斋馆“有朋亭”）。

❖ 株式会社小泉襖纸加工所

小泉幸雄

小泉幸雄先生的父亲是“唐纸师”，父亲在作坊里埋头工作的背影在他幼小的心灵里留下了深刻的印象。懂事后，他慢慢地帮着干活，不知不觉地也入了这一行，过了30岁后觉得自己已在作坊中顶了“半边天”。2001年2月，父子俩都被认定为国家传统工艺师。如今，小泉幸雄先生和儿子每天兢兢业业干着这份手艺活，他说：“虽然手艺还及不上父亲，但每天都想着要干出最好的活来。”

Yukio Koizumi grew up watching his father, a master karakami artisan, working in his shop. Once he began helping his father, it was just a short step to a career in the profession. By the time he reached 30, was already responsible for half of the shop's output. Father and son were recognized together as traditional craftsmen by the government of Japan in February 2001.

株式会社小泉襖纸加工所

- 东京都文京区汤岛1-10-13
- 株式会社小泉襖纸加工所　03-3816-0925
- 株式会社东京松屋展厅　03-3842-3785
- www.tokyomatsuya.co.jp

Photo/阿部kanori

浮世绘版画使用樱木，现代版画使用桦树木。
为了获得理想的色彩，要在制版底稿上反复刷颜料。

EDO MOKUHANGA
江户版画

版画历史悠久，大约在1200年以前随着佛教一起从中国传到日本，一开始是作为一种印刷技术用来翻刻佛经和佛像的。

江户时代中期，铃木晴信发明了被称为“锦绘”的多色印刷，画师、雕版师和印匠三方协作，制作出“浮世绘”。到了明治、大正年间，印刷的机械化程度提高使得版画印刷一时衰落，但版画作为一种传统工艺，其绚烂的艺术性在海外得到很高的评价，由此带来了它的东山再起。

如今，版画这一古老的艺术在世界上已广为人知。

Colorful woodblock prints, or hanga, are the culmination of centuries of development. Originally developed in China, woodblock printing came to Japan with the arrival of Buddhist missionaries from China, and began with the printing of Buddhist holy scriptures. It reached its pinnacle in the mid-Edo Period with the birth of the ukiyo-e or "floating world" -rich multicolor compositions illustrating the urban lifestyle of the time. Although woodblock printing eventually fell into decline, it became a highly valued art form overseas, and remains an international symbol of Japan.

上图／喷雾器和四色颜料。
下图／上色是最难的一道工序，以致于有“版画匠人为上色掉泪”的说法。
　　要调出一种称为“丼鼠色”的颜色，需要多年积累的经验。

上图／完成的作品悬空挂在作坊里晾干。
下图／做到这一步，需要花费相当多的时间和劳力。

竹皮刷
竹皮刷是版画师的命根子。有一种说法："逃难时，最先要带走的就是竹皮刷。"这是米田先生自己用竹皮和棉线做成的竹皮刷。

❖ 米田版画工房

米田良二

米田良二先生出生于1962年，是东京木版画工艺协会会员、重要民族文化遗产保存技术保护者、浮世绘木版画翻刻印刷技术保存协会会员、练马区传统工艺会会员。1980年，他开始师从父亲米田稔学艺，从未停止。1994年，他获得东京都青年优秀技能者知事奖。时至今日，米田良二先生钻研技艺已有30多年，但他仍热切地说："学无止境，至死方休。"米田版画工房的业务涉及版画、雕刻、印刷、碑帖拓印等，除了企划、制作外，还开设版画培训学校。

Ryoji Yoneda studied under the guidance of his father, Minoru, from 1980. By 1994 he was honored with a youth award for artistic excellence by the governor of Tokyo. Although he has now trained and worked for over 30 years, Yoneda is only beginning: he speaks of his training in the art as an ongoing process that will end only when he dies. At his workshop he is a one-man team, drawing the picture pattern, carving the woodblock to resemble the picture, then applying the ink to the woodblock for printing onto paper. When he is not working, he organizes projects and runs woodblock printing classes to further the art.

米田版画工房

东京都练马区丰玉南2-25-13-404
03-3994-3534

Photo/足立百合

TOKYO SHIPPO
东京景泰蓝

景泰蓝在日语中称作“七宝烧”，按古书记载，这七样宝指的是金、银、琉璃、水晶、琥珀、玛瑙、珍珠。之所以把景泰蓝称为“七宝烧”，意思是说这种器物就像这些金银珠宝一样高贵。

历史上确实有段时期是将上述七样金银珠宝弄碎后作为釉子来用的，后来随着技术的进步，人们就将有机金属（氯化银）掺入硅石中，使其产生七彩缤纷的颜色，做成了结实且更为漂亮的器物制品。

东京奥运会五环标志的胸章、领带夹、袖扣都是用景泰蓝制作的，最常见的是中小学的校徽，几乎人人都用到过这种工艺制品。

Shippo, the Japanese term for cloisonn literally means "seven jewels," referring to gold, silver, crystal, lapis lazuli, amber, agate and pearl, referenced in the Buddhist scriptures. The term likens the beauty of the enameling on metalwork to the priceless Seven Treasures. Well-known cloisonn products include pin-badges, tie pins and cuffs.

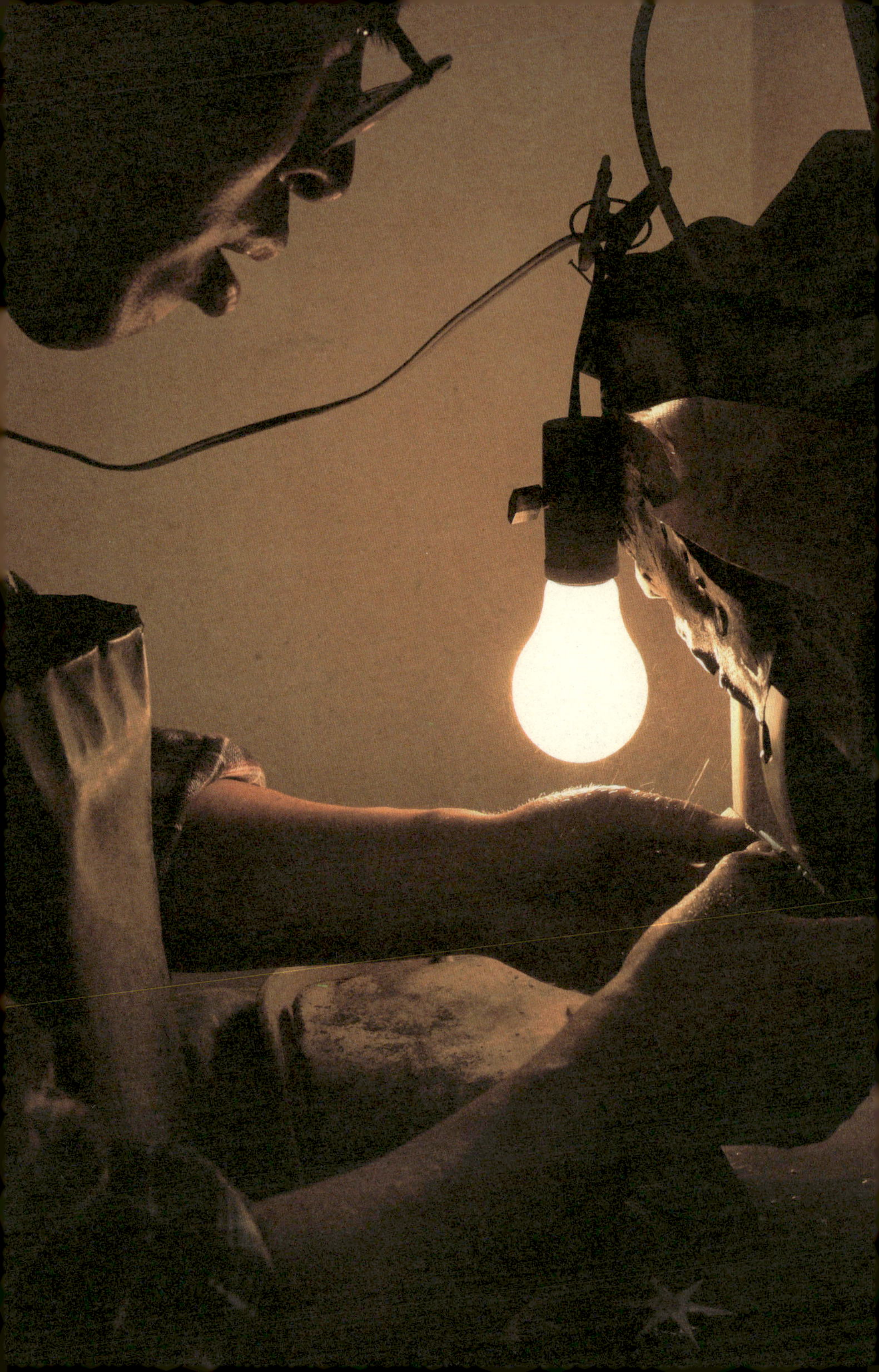

❖ 畠山景泰蓝制作所

畠山弘

畠山弘先生1953年出生在南千住，大学毕业后，为继承家业，他花了10年时间学习景泰蓝制作的基本技术，后来又掌握了景泰蓝产品设计，知识面更加宽泛。除了东京景泰蓝以外，他还进行其他景泰蓝的研究。2002年，东京景泰蓝被认定为东京都传统工艺；2004年，畠山弘先生获得景泰蓝原创门类东京都产业劳动局长奖。2005年，也就是他立志成为一名景泰蓝匠人的28年后，被认定为东京都传统工艺师。出自畠山弘先生之手的景泰蓝作品，其色彩变幻莫测、内涵丰富。

Hiroshi Hatakeyama was born in Minamisenju in 1953. After graduating from university, he joined the family business and spent ten years learning the fundamentals of enameling and metalwork, eventually mastering cloisonn design and production techniques. He was officially recognized as a Tokyo Master Traditional Craftsman in 2005 for his seemingly limitless skills with modern cloisonn

畠山景泰蓝制作所

东京都荒川区南千住5-43-4
03-3801-4844
www.tokyo-shippou.com

Photo/濑尾纯子

EDO GARASU
江户玻璃

日本的玻璃生产可追溯至弥生时代，虽然后来曾一度中断，但接着从葡萄牙、中国又传来了玻璃生产技艺，生产出玻璃器皿、玻璃艺术品等手工玻璃制品。

明治时代以后，日本的玻璃生产主要以东京为中心，现在在东京都内也分布有好多个手工玻璃生产作坊。

随着工业化步伐的加快，东京都涌现出一批吸收欧洲技术、制作技艺高超的匠人。他们每天在玻璃炉窑旁同高温作战，源源不断地生产出各种手工玻璃作品。

Glass production started in the Yayoi Period in Japan, but died out for a time until it was revived in the 17th century with vitrified glass products including bidoro and giyaman. Later, European glass technology was introduced and combined with indigenous Japanese techniques. Today, glassmaking artisans employ highly sophisticated skills to produce glass products of superb quality, as well as handmade works of art with applications in a variety of areas.

❖田岛玻璃株式会社

小西和男

入行已有40年的小西和男先生称得上是手工玻璃制作的高手。玻璃制作方法有“吹制法”“型制法”等多种，但不管哪一种制作方法，都需要有多年积累下的经验养成的高超技术。

一气呵成的多道制作工序由数名匠人组成的小组完成，而身怀绝技的小西和男先生作为头牌匠人，也每天奋战在生产第一线。工作间隙，他还悉心指导新人后辈，深受年轻人爱戴。人们评价小西和男先生的作品不仅技术水平高超，还极富艺术性。

With 40 years experience, Kazuo Konishi is an acclaimed leader in his field, renowned for his artistry as well as his unsurpassed workmanship. Nevertheless, he continues working tirelessly to hone his skills further. When he is not actually creating glasswork, he is helping aspiring craftsmen with technical instruction.

田岛玻璃株式会社

东京都江户川区松江4-18-8（总部）

03-3652-2727

www.tajimaglass.com

Photo/纪彰雄

先在桂木上开好一个个孔，然后将一束一束刷毛仔细植入孔中，
要尽量使每一束刷毛一样齐整，这需要匠人具有相当熟练的技巧。

TOKYO TEUEBURASHI
东京手植刷

日本最古老的刷子是用来涂漆的工具（记载于公元923年出版的《和妙类聚抄》），而西式刷子首次传到日本则是在1877年，在当年举行的第一届国内劝业博览会上展出了法国出产的刷子。

工厂的机械化程度提高后，刷子便成批成批地被大量生产出来，但是用手工方式将一束一束刷毛仔细植入制作的刷子比机器植入的刷子更经久耐用。刷子匠人用灵巧的双手凭着熟练的技术制作的手植刷子至今仍有着顽强的生命力。

The first brushes of this variety were French-made items that appeared at an exposition held in 1877. Soon centers of brush manufacture arose in Japan, and mechanization eventually brought about mass production of the brushes. However, the bristles in hand-flocked brushes are more densely packed than their machine-made counterparts. They are stronger, and last longer.

❖ 有限会社平野刷子制作所

平野佳辉

大学一毕业，平野佳辉先生就继承了家业，在父亲也是师傅的平野道孝手下干着生产刷子的活儿。当时涂饰工程必定要用到油漆刷子，所以市场需求很旺盛。但是随着时代的发展，刷子行业慢慢就变得不景气了，平野刷子制作所也开始转向生产衣刷等家用刷子，亮出“平野的刷子”这一品牌，在全国进行产品推广销售。平野出产的刷子在制作上坚持传统工艺，用料上讲究采用天然材料，就算如此，他们还是注意倾听顾客真实的想法，努力制作出更轻便实用的手植刷子。

Upon graduation from university, Yoshiteru Hirano joined the family business under the tutelage of his father, Michitaka. At the time, there was a strong demand for painting brushes, but the painting industry has since declined. In response, the family expanded the business domain to include other products, such as clothing brushes. They manufacture and sell the line of brushes under the "Hirano Brushes" brand, which they also display in exhibitions across Japan.

有限会社平野刷子制作所

东京都足立区西绫濑1-2-23
03-3852-5440
www.burashiya.com

Photo/足立百合

东京雕金

东京手染浴衣

图书在版编目(CIP)数据

东京手艺人 / (日) Beretta P-05著; 杜海清译
.--上海: 文汇出版社, 2017. 7
ISBN 978-7-5496-2181-1
Ⅰ.①东… Ⅱ.①B… ②杜… Ⅲ.①手工业者-访问记-日本-现代 Ⅳ.①K833.138.1

中国版本图书馆CIP数据核字(2017)第144238号

著作权合同登记号: 图字 09-2017-450号

东京手艺人

作　　者 / Beretta P-05
译　　者 / 杜海清
责任编辑 / 戴铮
装帧设计 / 智勇

出 版 人 / 桂国强

出版发行 / 文汇出版社 (上海市威海路755号 邮政编码200041)
印刷装订 / 苏州市越洋印刷有限公司
版　　次 / 2018年4月第1版
印　　次 / 2018年4月第1次印刷
开　　本 / 889×1194 1/32
字　　数 / 80千字
印　　张 / 8
书　　号 / ISBN 978-7-5496-2181-1
定　　价 / 88.00元